THE
ENTREPRENEUR'S
OATH

First Edition

Rajesh D. Mudholkar, ACMA

Intellipi Publishing
Pune, India
ISBN Pending

and

Printed at:
Mudranik Technologies Pvt. Ltd
Bengaluru, India

This work is dedicated to my late father who stood as a living example of tenacity, optimism and mercifulness towards human fallibility even while enforcing discipline. He inspired me to aim high, pursue dreams with passion, and instilled the values of spiritedly overcoming any adversities that may come along.

Acknowledgements

This book is my third, after the first two which were based on my research in financial economics 'The Timeless Essence of Financial Science' and 'Value Erosion', published in 2013. The inspiration for this book came from a need to connect the larger, very existence of a business enterprise, with the financial economics required to run it.

I wish to express my gratitude to God, whose blessings has always been with me, Lipika my wife, who has not only been the biggest source of inspiration and my best critic, but also contributed to enhancing my understanding about human relationships. Being a husband to her and a father to my daughter Raashi has tremendously enriched me with a holistic view towards life.

I am thankful to all my friends, well wishers, acquaintances, colleagues and students who motivated me with their appreciation for my work. I consider every single person with whom I have interacted during the creation of this work for various purposes - be it discussing a point, seeking advice, or simply bouncing off ideas - as a valuable contributor towards the end result. I wish to sincerely thank each one of them.

Rajesh D. Mudholkar, Author

Disclaimer

Utmost care has been taken to ensure factual accuracy of data used and/or presented in this book. Errors and omissions if any, that might have crept in despite rigorous efforts, are purely accidental and unintentional. The sources from where such data are obtained have been cited as footnotes on corresponding pages for easy reference and due credit has been given to the original copyright owner. The analyses and arguments presented here, are only intended to be an objective critique from a professional viewpoint with due respects to their learned authors, originators or creators. There is no intention to offend any of them, whether living or dead. This book is purely an analytical treatise to promote new thought, based on the author's own work and ideas, and not to be construed as professional advice.

Rajesh D. Mudholkar, Author.

Table of Contents

Preface

Is there any secret formula? For anyone who aspires to be an exemplary business leader, this one thought would have certainly baffled the mind at some point in time along the career. Most would have undergone some or the other formal business management education. Many would have delved into biographies of great business leaders to search for the secrets of powerful leadership.

Even though thousands of people study the same thing and apply the knowledge gained in their work places, why is it that only a small number become extraordinary leaders and their organizations admired and respected in society? Of all that is learnt in typical business management programs - accounting, finance, marketing, human resource management, economics, project management, strategy and a host of other hard and soft skills - what is it that makes for a winning combination that shapes a person and the organization he or she leads, into iconic figures that everyone wants to emulate? None!

Dyslexic as a child and with poor academic performance as a student, this boy's headmaster once told him he would either end up in prison or become a millionaire. He defied both outcomes, turning out to be among the top ten richest citizens of the United Kingdom, with an estimated net worth of nearly US$5 billion according to the Forbes 2012 list of billionaires[1], and was 'Knighted' by Her Majesty Queen Elizabeth II of England in 1999 for his 'services to entrepreneurship'.[2] Leave alone an MBA degree to flaunt, he did not even earn an ordinary university graduation degree, nor did he inherit any family business. His father was only a barrister. The profile page on Forbes list of world's billionaires shows his education as: 'Drop Out, High

---

[1] http://en.wikipedia.org/wiki/Richard_Branson
[2] http://www.businessweek.com/stories/2007-07-25/richard-bransons-latest-venturebusinessweek-business-news-stock-market-and-financial-advice

School.'[3] This iconic, dyslexic turned knighted tycoon is Sir Richard Branson, the founder of Virgin Group, comprising more than 400 companies operating worldwide.

If that doesn't hold you in awe, what you are about to read will. According to Levinson Medical Center for Learning Disabilities™, based in New York, "Dyslexia is a syndrome of multiple varied reading and non-reading symptoms affecting over 40 million American children and adults. Many with dyslexia and related learning and attention disorders realize quite early that they are not like their peers. Their learning and coordination, or klutzy difficulties, often lead to impaired self-esteem, ridicule, being bullied and even bullying. They often feel dumb, depressed, and isolated. As a result, one can sadly wonder just how many gifted and creative dyslexics have been blocked from fulfilling their genetic destinies and potential. All too often, learning-

---

[3] http://www.forbes.com/profile/richard-branson/

disabled children grow up to be underemployed adults, shunted into routine, dead-end occupations for life. Some have difficulties maintaining families and raising children properly. Many drift into drugs and alcohol and even crime. Their loss and cost to society is incalculable."

Richard Branson was not the one to be bogged down by his condition. He discovered quickly that he was endowed with one extraordinary ability - the art of connecting with people! Dr. Levinson says about Richard Branson: "his gifted interpersonal and business talents drove him to succeed."[4]

Can you comprehend even in your wildest dreams a business enterprise without the presence of 'human beings' to run it? Further, regardless of the number of robotic equipments, sophisticated electronic data management systems and the best of people available and willing to contribute their talents, can

---

[4] http://www.dyslexiaonline.com/basics/famous_dyslexics.html

there be any business activity without 'customers'? Above all, despite everything being 'well managed', if 'society' and the 'ecosystem' - the very arena within which all businesses exist, woefully degenerate, will any business be able to sustain itself? Be it employees, customers or society, everything that happens in the world of business involves 'people'.

Economic science, the cornerstone of trade and commerce, tells us that the entrepreneur is like the catalyst in a chemical reaction. He is the single most important economic agent who deploys 'labor' to work on 'land and other physical resources' to produce goods and services that 'consumers' need. The third economic factor 'capital' or 'money' only acts as a medium of exchange, a measure and store of value and a standard unit of account, necessary to complete and sustain the value creation cycle, sometimes infinitely.

The value chain involves transformation of one form of value into another. All components making up the value chain ultimately reduce to four key elements - employees, customers, society and the ecosystem. If there's a holy grail of great business, it is embedded in this quartet. All that is needed is to peel away superficial layers and tune the four to operate in rhythm.

This book is not a self-help guide, nor is it a pedantic business discourse or any book of 'secrets'. It is intended to be a provocative exploration. It raises questions and stokes the reader into asking questions, and through the interconnected strands it follows, it leads to the discovery that successful businesses thrive and become great over time only by adopting a caring and conscientious approach towards employees, towards customers and towards society and the physical environment at large - the ecosystem, quite like a physician towards his patients.

We all know that healthcare professionals must take the Hippocratic Oath, swearing to uphold high standards of ethics in their practice. The modern version of the oath varies between countries and differs from the original, believed to have been either written or inspired in late 5th century B.C by the ancient Greek physician Hippocrates, who is regarded as the father of western medicine. The spirit of the original oath covers several areas which physicians are expected to swear to. Beginning with a commitment to the Greek Gods of healing, it includes promises of ethical conduct towards teachers, students, patients and peers, and of being virtuous and to exercise discretion.[5]

Similarly, anyone assuming a position of public leadership, such as the head of a country or its Chief Justice, also has to take an oath, swearing to uphold the spirit of the 'Constitution' and the 'Laws of the land'. Even Kings in ancient times were, and

---

[5] http://en.wikipedia.org/wiki/Hippocratic_Oath

contemporary Monarchs still are officially sworn-in in a 'Coronation' ceremony. So are athletes and their coaches representing a country, as well as the judges, required to take the Olympic Oath at opening ceremonies of the Olympic Games.[6]

Interestingly, Sir Joseph Rotblat, a Polish physicist, who was conferred the 1995 Nobel Peace Prize for his contribution towards nuclear disarmament, suggested a Hippocratic Oath for Scientists, to inculcate courage, rigour, honesty and integrity among the scientific community, and to ensure that any adverse effects their work may have on people, animals or the natural environment, is minimized and not justified away.[7]

The Hippocratic Oath taken by medical practitioners concludes with a promise to follow what is being sworn and thus be respected by society; and in the event of its violation, face adverse consequences and

---

[6] http://en.wikipedia.org/wiki/Olympic_Oath
[7] http://en.wikipedia.org/wiki/Hippocratic_Oath_for_Scientists

social humiliation. However, there's no punishment prescribed for violation of the oath per se except in many cases, practitioners being stripped of their licence. Its compliance gets indirectly covered under civil and criminal laws worldwide. Yet regardless of each country's own laws, the Hippocratic Oath anchors the conscience of medical practitioners to an implied moral diktat.

I remember being a 'boy-scout' in school when all new inducts were officially sworn-in with an oath. Every meeting also began with a recital of the same oath that went like this:

"On my honour, I promise that I will do my best to do my duty to God and my country, to help other people at all times and to obey the Scout Law."

At the time, none of us never really understood that being a Scout was really about character building. We did all that was told, because most of those community service activities were a lot of fun. There were no 'internet-games' or 'social-media' then, to 'distract' us. But the spirit of honesty and service to people and country that the scouting movement inculcated and promoted, earned Robert Baden Powell, its founder, the title of 'Lord of Gilwell' in 1929 conferred by the British King. From the first experimental camp he organized in 1907 with only 20 boys, the movement has transformed today into more than 40 million Scouts of all ages, both male and female, in over 200 countries and territories. The World Organization of the Scout Movement (WOSM), that serves the 'Scout Movement' today, has as its main purpose, the task of promoting the last message left by Lord Baden Powell: "Try and leave this world a little better than you found it".[8] Pursuing this goal is far more relevant in today's world than it ever was.

---

[8] http://scout.org/

If an oath has the tacit power to stir the conscience and act as a moral lever to drive ethical conduct, will an entrepreneurial oath make a difference to the way business is done? Even if such an oath is not prescribed or imposed, shouldn't every entrepreneur and business leader embrace it as a voluntary onus? Or are we going to argue that if it was necessary, then the pioneers of capitalism would have introduced it anyway? After all, the Hippocratic Oath already existed during the industrial revolution to serve as an inspiration!

Have we ever seen placards or heard 'Thanks for coming' or 'Welcome again', when we visit our trusted family doctor? But we still always go to the same good soul every time the need arises, don't we? And doctors don't expect tax incentives for abiding by the 'Hippocratic Oath', do they? Therein lies the answer. There's no other 'secret'.

As far as I can see, we are on the wrong cliff!

1

Zoom Out,
Look Far!

"We don't want this globalised economic system which does us so much harm. Men and women have to be at the centre (of an economic system) as God wants, not money."
- Pope Francis

Celebrating Mass for thousands of people outside the cathedral in Cagliari, the capital of Sardinia, Pope Francis made - what 'The Telegraph (U.K) reported as - "one of his strongest attacks yet on the global economic system"[1]. The Pope was responding to the capital's youth unemployment rate of about 51 per cent, an inevitable fallout of

---

[1] http://www.telegraph.co.uk/news/religion/the-pope/10327227/Pope-tells-big-business-not-to-worship-the-god-of-money.html

economic crisis that gripped most of the island's mining and industrial sectors, not withstanding the fact that it clocked the highest per capita income - €16,837 as of 2012 - in Southern Italy[2]. Sardinia is the second largest island in the Mediterranean Sea and an autonomous region of Italy. However, Pope Francis was not referring to Sardinia alone. The same problems existed in the rest of Europe and beyond, he said.

Did the architects of 'Industrial Revolution' ever envisage, that lurking within what was termed as - 'a psychological change in man's confidence, in his ability to use resources and to master nature'[3] - was a grave danger of abuse, that could bring misery to humankind nearly two centuries later?

The transformation brought about by the industrial revolution - from manual production to machines,

[2] http://en.wikipedia.org/wiki/Sardinia
[3] http://www.britannica.com/EBchecked/topic/287086/Industrial-Revolution

new processes for production of chemicals and iron, more extensive use of steam power, development of machine tools and change from bio-fuels to coal - led economic historians to believe that the onset of the Industrial Revolution was the most important event in the history of humanity since the domestication of animals and plants.

The change was not without debate though; but, not much unlike several irrelevant yet frenzied conflicts seen in contemporary world, much of those revolved around the appropriateness of using the word 'revolution'. Arguments came forth and continue even now from some historians, whether or not the process of economic and social change took place gradually or was truly abrupt enough to qualify as a 'revolution'. No matter which direction debates took, one thing did not fail consensus. To quote Nobel Laureate Robert E. Lucas, Jr., "For the first time in history, the living standards of the masses of ordinary people have begun to undergo sustained growth...Nothing remotely like this economic behavior is mentioned by the classical economists, even as a theoretical possibility "[4]

The euphoric optimism inspired by the accomplishments would have been completely understandable as much as it would have been a natural consequence of the social change that also occurred. Around the same time that the Industrial Revolution spread from Britain to the rest of the world - circa 1760 to 1840, a cultural movement took shape in Europe to reform society that was steeped in ideas grounded in tradition and faith, to one driven by scientific thought, skepticism, and intellectual interchange. This 'Age of Enlightenment' as it was called, created the idea of 'Laissez-faire', an economic system unhindered by the restrictions of government. Laissez-faire originated in the eighteenth-century France, and built on by other economists. The underlying belief was that, in

---

[4] http://en.wikipedia.org/wiki/Industrial_Revolution

following their selfish interests, individuals would contribute positively to society through what was understood as the 'trickle effect'. Since this natural order (as they viewed it) functioned successfully without government intervention, they advocated the abolishment of unnecessary laws, limiting state involvement towards protecting the rights of private property and individual liberty and for removal of artificial trade barriers.[5]

Now, in the 21st century, that the incremental benefits of both, industrialization and the laissez-faire system are seriously undermined by the rapidly deteriorating socio-economic conditions, it warrants serious introspection and a major course correction in the way business is done. No amount of exhortation to this effect would be deemed to be an overstated paranoia or figments of imagination emerging from deranged minds of economic laggards, because the blunt truth making the world's

---

[5] http://en.wikipedia.org/wiki/Laissez-faire

socio-economic health increasingly pallid has already exposed itself in more than one international forum. Global centers of leadership and other watchdog bodies are already expressing fear and anguish about a horrid future for the planet and its natives, if any more time is lost in denial, debate and buck-passing.

There cannot be a more opportune time for change than a crisis, just as much as necessity gives birth to invention. In his acclaimed book 'The Argumentative Indian' published in 2005, Nobel Laureate and Professor of Economics and Philosophy at Harvard University, Dr. Amartya Sen aptly highlighted the need for social introspection now. Quoting Oxford philosopher Jonathan Glover's writing in 'Moral History of the Twentieth Century', he says "we must not only reflect on what has happened in the last century, but also 'need to look hard and clearly at some monsters inside us' and to consider ways and means of 'caging and taming them'. The end of a century - and of a millennium - is certainly a good moment to engage in critical examinations of this kind"[6]

Introspection is indeed the key to knowledge and understanding. Yet, the ecologically sensitive events that have unfolded before this generation, rapidly deteriorating it in the recent past, don't fail to evoke as much a sense of worry if not more, as the euphoria induced by the industrial revolution, but remedial actions seem only to trudge along.

Has the human race failed to pause, understand and introspect whether the living standards of ordinary people truly experienced sustained growth in the manner that was contemplated with the onset of the industrial revolution? Or has the high-speed, multi-tasking and big-data crunching culture insulated us from hearing the rumble of impending disaster? Have we unwittingly succumbed like stupefied prey to the monsters inside us, instead of taming them?

---

[6] Amartya Sen, The Argumentative Indian, Penguin Books, pg 273

Worse than anything, have we deliberately chosen to turn a blind eye towards several dangerous ill effects that are too obvious to be neglected, because of a delusionary reckless pursuit of large immediate economic benefits over real sustainability? Are we guilty of discarding the garb of moral conscience, and have no qualms strutting around in our denuded state?

With the industrial revolution two and a half centuries behind us, and the trail of damage - inching towards near critical - too conspicuous to be ignored, the apparent lackadaisical response for restoring socio-economic balance fails to inspire enough conviction to detract us from a deep sense of despondency about our economic future.

This is not to say that all capitalism deserves abhorrence, or that only an alternate economic system guarantees human welfare. While the self-interest driven 'natural order' of a 'laissez-faire' system was believed to contribute to social good[7], the strongest of all criticisms - against corporate capitalism in particular - has been the fear that it will lead to depletion of the earth's finite natural resources and cause environmental degradation[8].

Even if the actions towards perseveration of natural wealth and restoration of its loss alone gather sufficient urgency, it would spur enough momentum for rectifying other related socio-economic ills because of the mass social awakening it would induce. It is not capitalism per se, but its unintended consequences that need correction. The evidence however, is pointing in the adverse direction and still faces the challenge of breaking through barriers put up by detractors.

Pointing to the tragic apathy even in the face of imminent catastrophe, Nobel Laureate Paul

[7] Fine, Sidney. Laissez Faire and the General-Welfare State. United States: The University of Michigan Press, 1964
[8] McMurty, John (1999). The Cancer Stage of Capitalism. Pluto Press. ISBN 0-7453-1347-7

Krugman wrote in a column in The New York Times in 2009 "I started thinking about boiled frogs recently as I watched the depressing state of debate over both economic and environmental policy.....if the consensus of the economic experts is grim, the consensus of the climate experts is utterly terrifying. At this point, the central forecast of leading climate models - not the worst-case scenario but the most likely outcome - is utter catastrophe, a rise in temperatures that will totally disrupt life as we know it, if we continue along our present path.[9]"

What is the grim reality? Although capitalism has increased global trade, the resultant myopic pursuit of profits has also increased worldwide poverty, turning the glorious dream of socio-economic uplift due to 'laissez-faire' into not merely a mirage but worse - a living nightmare. Alan Greenspan, who served as Chairman of the United States Federal Reserve from 1987 to 2006 told the United States

---

[9] http://www.nytimes.com/2009/07/13/opinion/13krugman.html?_r=0

Congress while responding to the 2007 financial crisis, "The whole intellectual edifice collapsed. I made a mistake in presuming that the self-interests of organizations, specifically banks and others, were such that they were best capable of protecting their own shareholders. ... I was shocked."

Whether intentional or accidental, if the custodians of investors' wealth fail in their duty to safeguard even the very means to their ends, it instills hardly any confidence, counting on them for doing the right things for protecting everything else connected with business. Rather, entrepreneurial losses because of imprudent financial management, becomes an excuse for cutting down legitimate rewards to other factors of production. In what can be called as institutional manifestation of Maslow's theory, higher goals take a back-seat because achievement of even basic goals falters. That only sets a vicious cycle in motion, dragging all stakeholders towards misery.

The disastrous demise of Lehman Brothers in 2008, India's leading wind-turbine maker Suzlon Energy struggling to recover from losses due to its huge debt burden, and Kingfisher Airlines unable to pay salaries to its employees while the employees are in no mood to listen to the promoter CEO's appeals for support, are only few examples of stakeholders' suffering. This is not to undermine the importance of eliminating wasteful expenses, or even to exercise austerity when the need arises, but to highlight the truth that in the long term only those businesses would be supported in adverse times by all stakeholders, who have been fair in their dealings with each one of them, consistently.

Pope Francis described unfettered capitalism as "a new tyranny" and exhorted world leaders to fight rising poverty and inequality, in his 'Evangelii

Gaudium' (English: The Joy of the Gospel), a 2013 apostolic exhortation.[10] In it he says:

"Some people continue to defend trickle-down theories which assume that economic growth, encouraged by a free market, will inevitably succeed in bringing about greater justice and inclusiveness in the world. This opinion, which has never been confirmed by the facts, expresses a crude and naive trust in the goodness of those wielding economic power and in the sacralized workings of the prevailing economic system. Meanwhile, the excluded are still waiting.[11]

If all the world's medical professionals practiced capitalism of the sort discussed above, would the profession retain its nobility? If an explicit 'Hippocratic Oath' was deemed necessary for good

---

[10] Naomi O'Leary (26 November 2013). Pope attacks 'tyranny' of markets in manifesto for papacy. Reuters.
[11] Zachary A. Goldfarb and Michelle Boorstein (26 November 2013). Pope Francis denounces 'trickle-down' economic theories in critique of inequality. The Washington Post.

medical practice to prevail, even where tacit trust in the goodness of those wielding healing power must exist by default, then a similar oath for ensuring good entrepreneurial practice shouldn't be an exaggerated proposition!

If this doesn't work, we'll shut down!

2

Not 'Human Resource', It's 'Human Beings'

Human intelligence 'peaked thousands of years ago and we've been on an intellectual and emotional decline ever since'
- Professor Gerald Crabtree, Stanford

Professor Gerald Crabtree, a leading geneticist who heads a genetics laboratory at Stanford University in California, made the above controversial hypothesis based on new developments in genetics, anthropology, and neurobiology. This was reported in November 2012 by one of United Kingdom's well known newspaper

'The Independent'[1]. Professor Crabtree believes that "the immense capacity of the human brain to learn new tricks is under attack from an array of genetic mutations that have accumulated since people started living in cities a few thousand years ago. Is the human species doomed to intellectual decline? Will our intelligence ebb away in centuries to come, leaving our descendants incapable of using the technology their ancestors invented? In short: will Homo be left without his sapiens?"

In a world trapped in the spin of a socio-economic whirlpool, where business doesn't cease to lament the scarcity of skills, pushing the blame on B-Schools and unable employ their students, while youth deter from pursuing business management studies because poor employment prospects drowns them in disillusionment, the shocking revelation of already deteriorated brain power only likely to

---

[1] http://www.independent.co.uk/news/science/human-intelligence-peaked-thousands-of-years-ago-and-weve-been-on-an-intellectual-and-emotional-decline-ever-since-8307101.html?origin=internalSearch

worsen, would put even the most seasoned human resource professional in a quandary. It's like driving in a car race with a steadily deteriorating vehicle on an increasingly challenging track.

The most benign among us would also be rendered helpless if the quagmire of catastrophe is allowed to strengthen its grip around us. Albert Camus the French Nobel Prize winning author, journalist, and philosopher warned about this outcome when he said "The evil that is in the world almost always comes of ignorance, and good intentions may do as much harm as malevolence if they lack understanding"[2].

Whether we become the proverbial boiled frogs or head-in-the-sand ostriches, deceiving ourselves with the gloss of our own perception of human development and accomplishments, or open the windows of our minds to understand where we really

---

[2] http://en.wikiquote.org/wiki/November_7

stand, is again a matter of intelligent choice. Making the wrong choice would only accelerate our intellectual and emotional decline. If Professor Gerald Crabtree's hypothesis is true, then we are truly flying into strong headwinds and need to navigate carefully. Have we reduced to shriveled versions of our ancestors, merely guarding ourselves like caretakers of dilapidated ruins of magnificent ancient monuments? It's not the janitors' duty to worry over how to reconstruct antique structures they are custodians of. That job requires higher competencies, which only visionary hands can provide.

If past damage cannot be undone, can we prevent worsening the future scenario? The best we can do is to preserve what we have and utilize its full potential. Excessive dependence on the 'conveniences' that technological developments provide us, perhaps leaves less room to hope for a reversal of human evolutionary decline, simply because those very technological aides that we have developed, makes the 'struggle for existence' - they key trigger for evolutionary growth - that much less intense.

Can human will and perseverance break through the limitations that adverse genetic mutation has put around us? Award-winning journalist Daniel Coyle writes in his book 'The Talent Code', how all of us can achieve our full 'potential' by training our brains in the right way. He explains how a neural insulator called myelin grows thicker with right practice, making neural signals carried by nerve fibres stronger and faster, resulting in extraordinary talent.[3] However, the fact remains that if the 'potential' itself has suffered evolutionary deterioration, even the most practiced-to-perfection talent would still fall short compared to what our ancestors could have achieved with similar training. 'Performance' would always be limited by 'Potential'.

---

[3] Daniel Coyle, The Talent Code', Arrow Books 2010, pg 5.

What implications does the foregoing have for 'Human Resource Development' practitioners? Undoubtedly, acquiring, nurturing, developing and rewarding talent, counts among the most critical functions of sound enterprise management. Understanding and managing people is also an essential quality leaders can't succeed without. Unless business leaders do the right things towards nurturing human capital, long term sustainability of business enterprises would be destined for doom.

The heart of any organization is 'people', whether in commercial business or in public life. Are there any decipherable signals that indicate illness brewing beneath apparent strength? Research shows there are. Truly contented employees have turned out to be rare species. In an article published in May 2012, Forbes reported the findings of an online snapshot survey of 411 workers in the U.S and Canada by 'Right Management' - a subsidiary of the giant staffing firm 'ManpowerGroup' - which showed that nearly two-thirds of American employees were not happy at work. If that could have been too narrow a sample to be representative, a previous survey of 30,000 employees worldwide carried out by Mercer in 2011 showed that "between 28% and 56% of employees in 17 spots around the globe wanted to leave their jobs", the Forbes report said.[4] If that was still not convincing enough, another massive survey by Gallup in 2013, covering 230,000 workers in 142 countries - also reported by Forbes - made shocking revelations, saying:

"there are twice as many 'actively disengaged' workers in the world as there are 'engaged' workers who love their jobs...Only 13% of workers feel a sense of passion for their work, a deep connection to their employer and they spend their days driving innovation and moving their company forward...The vast majority, some 63%, are unhappy...They sleepwalk through their days, putting little energy

---

[4] http://www.forbes.com/sites/susanadams/2012/05/18/new-survey-majority-of-employees-dissatisfied/

into their work. A full 24% hate their jobs. They act out and undermine what their coworkers accomplish....the last two categories (adding to 87%)...are emotionally disconnected from their workplaces and less likely to be productive....In other words, work is more often a source of frustration than one of fulfillment for nearly 90% of the world's workers." [5]

That was a view only from one side of the fence. How does the scenario look from the employers' perspective? Mercer's 'Talent Barometer Survey-2012'[6] that included responses from HR and talent management executives of 1,268 organizations from a wide variety of industries, representing 65 countries around the globe, observes:

"To deliver top value to the organization, talent must have the skills and knowledge necessary for the

[5] http://www.forbes.com/sites/susanadams/2013/10/10/unhappy-employees-outnumber-happy-ones-by-two-to-one-worldwide/
[6] http://www.mercer.com/talent-rising-summary

role, as well as the broader creative and critical-thinking skills that can elevate organizational performance to its highest level. Despite high unemployment in many regions of the world, organizations today face a shortfall of qualified talent to fill critical roles."

One of the key findings of the survey was "57% of the organizations said that educational institutions are failing to generate the talent needed by their businesses today, and 59% believe this still will be true three to five years out."

Another survey, the 2012-13 'Global Talent Management and Rewards Study' conducted by Towers Watson[7], a leading global professional services company, also shares the industry's concern regarding scarcity of skills. The survey was fielded across 29 markets around the world, eliciting

---

[7] http://www.towerswatson.com/en/Insights/IC-Types/Survey-Research-Results/2012/09/2012-Global-Talent-Management-and-Rewards-Study

responses from more than 32,000 full-time workers across a range of industries and functions. The survey found the following.

"Almost three-quarters of survey respondents (72%), cite problems attracting critical-skill employees. About six in 10 have difficulty attracting high potential and top-performing workers (60% and 59% respectively)."

A third survey, the '2013-Talent Shortage Survey'[8] - which covered over 38,000 employers across 42 countries and territories - conducted by ManpowerGroup, says:

"As is becoming clear in the Human Age, securing access to the increasingly finite pool of individuals with in-demand skill sets will be fundamental to business success".

---

[8] http://www.manpowergroup.com/wps/wcm/connect/587d2b45-c47a-4647-a7c1-e7a74f68fb85/2013_Talent_Shortage_Survey_Results_US_high+res.pdf?MOD=AJPERES

The findings of this survey echoes what the former two surveys revealed, saying:

"35% of over 38,000 employers surveyed report they are experiencing difficulty filling jobs due to lack of available talent. This......is the highest proportion of employers expressing concern about talent shortages since 2007..........more than one out of five employers report that they are currently doing nothing to remedy the skills gaps, indicating that they may not understand how the talent shortage is putting their business at risk or they simply don't know how to effectively solve the issue"

Broadly, both perspectives point to a common surmise that neither employees nor employers are happy with each other! Are all employees - regardless of rank - not happy because lack of required skills affects their performance, their interpersonal relationships and consequently organizational performance? Or do senior organizational leaders find employees in the lower ranks alone lacking in required skills, causing a stressful therefore unhappy work environment? A third situation involving an exact reversal of the second could also be possible - high potential, eager to learn executives may not find the right mentors and role models in their bosses.

No matter where the shoe pinches, only the wearer can identify the exact spot - provided he stops running. If he happens to be the leader of a pack where everyone is running with ill-fitting shoes but no one complains, one can imagine how painfully the pack would trudge along because no one wants to be the only one complaining and each one fears being singled out from the team or be blamed for antagonizing the leader! Worse would be the case if only the leader knows the destination and the route.

Organizational values and culture must first be lived in its true spirit by the leader, before it could trickle-down the entire structure. The identity of most business organizations is defined by their 'Vision' and 'Mission' statements. Many also have elaborate written policies specifying the company's culture, behavior and ethical standards. Do all employees across the hierarchy understand their companies' vision, mission and values? If most do, it's an indisputable indicator of good organizational health, and of senior management being effective in their communication. It shows they have taken the effort to not only set the sail in the right direction but also to provide navigational maps to all. Is it possible to aim right if the target isn't in clear sight?

Unfortunately, various surveys show that the truth is far from ideal. Employees are unsure of their companies' vision and values. "Only 42% of employees know their organization's vision, mission, and values. That's an alarmingly low number. Too many executives are not communicating and reinforcing their company's guiding principles and mission." This was the finding of a survey by

'Tinypulse', an employee engagement company, based on the analysis of 40,000 responses from 300 global organisations.[9] The respondents were asked whether they could recite their organizations' vision, mission and values.

A similar conclusion was reported in a Harvard Business Review (June 2013) article titled "When CEOs Talk Strategy, Is Anyone Listening?" The report wrote about researchers at the University of Technology in Sydney who asked employees of 20 major Australian corporations with clearly articulated public strategies to identify their employer's strategy from among six choices. Only 29% answered correctly.[10] More disturbing than the fact that respondents were unable to identify what was shown, is quite surprisingly, the following comment made by HBR which dangerously underrates the ills of unclear goals; it refers to the findings as "...good

---

9 https://www.tinypulse.com/employee-engagement-survey-2013
10 http://hbr.org/2013/06/when-ceos-talk-strategy-is-anyone-listening/ar/1

news: The firms in the sample are all high performers, suggesting that a company can thrive even if employees are clueless about its long-term vision." The only comment on this response is - if you disbelieve the need for goal clarity, try walking around a familiar room with your eyes shut without bumping into anything.

Most people, by not being aware of why their company exists in the first place - something that vision, mission and values statements define - are unwittingly out of sync with their companies' strategic direction. Downplaying this handicap is like following a medication regimen prescribed by your doctor that keeps you healthy, without really understanding how and what those medicines are doing to your body. You are clueless, yet healthy! Every discomfort would compel consulting the doctor, even if it happens to be something harmless or mere side-effect of medicines. Imagine the musicians of the London Philharmonic Orchestra, each one playing their own sheet pieces perfectly and in sync with the rest, but none of them except the conductor heard the entire composition even once beforehand. Wouldn't the orchestra perform with far more finesse if they had?

Emphasizing the absolute responsibility of senior leadership to clearly define and communicate their organizations' strategic direction, Jimmy Leppert, an engagement leader at Kotter International succinctly explains in an article in Forbes (July 2013), titled 'When CEOs Talk Strategy, 70% Of The Company Doesn't Get It', why employees who are misaligned with their company's strategic direction, can drag the company down.[11]

Can the same set of people perform differently on different tracks laid by their leaders? If leadership includes the capacity to identify and activate unknown strengths in people, the answer is yes.

---

[11] http://www.forbes.com/sites/johnkotter/2013/07/09/heres-why-ceo-strategies-fall-on-deaf-ears/

'Unknown' refers to even those strengths which fall in the 'blind-spot' and the more difficult 'unknown' quadrant of Johari window. The Johari window is a cognitive psychology tool developed by two American psychologists, Joseph Luft and Harrington Ingham in 1955 to help in understanding interpersonal relationships.[12] 'Blind-spot' is one of the quadrants of the window that refers to the cognitive area not known to self but known to others, while the 'unknown' quadrant is neither known to self nor to others. The key to leading human action towards extra-ordinary performance could lie in these two areas, which a visionary leader must explore.

Doing the right things to get the 'people power' work for organizational success requires thinking about 'people' as more than mere 'human resource', a commodity like any other factor of production. The best example of a leader's capability to galvanize

---

[12] http://en.wikipedia.org/wiki/Johari_window

trust and following among people is seen in the story published in 'The Boston Globe' titled 'Market Basket CEO gets reprieve' (July 18, 2013)[13]. The story was about Arthur T. Demoulas, CEO of 'DeMoulas Super Markets, Inc.', a private 96 year old company operating a chain of more than 70 supermarkets by the brand name 'Market Basket', based in Massachusetts. When the board held a meeting to consider firing Demoulas - taking a two-decade family feud over management and ownership of the company to extremes - more than 44,000 employees and supporters signed a petition to retain him, and hundreds of employees chanted in support at the venue of the meeting. "He's the most honorable man I've ever met - loyal to his customers and employees," one of the directors who worked at the company for decades said. "I don't think you'll find another company where the CEO cares this much about his customers and employees," said the

---

13

http://www.bostonglobe.com/2013/07/18/marketbasket/qKpk8JGaLs
mUmLwJ0oItHL/story.html

wife of another employee who had worked at the company for 30 years.

The only factor that catapults a leader above stereo-type 'performance yardsticks' and truly connect with employees, is extraordinary emotional intelligence. A great deal of intuitive and perceptive understanding of human beings coming from the leader builds strong bonds and helps people discover their strengths - their true potential. And that's the key to peak individual performance, excellent camaraderie and as a result of both, a great organization. Keep the stereo-type 'performance' yardsticks aside, look at tapping 'potential' that many times lies hidden, and which is the root cause of employee dissatisfaction. Real communication does not stop at sending out routine fact sheets and memos. A CEO living the company's vision in every respect, and demonstrating excellence in his own body language, behavior, performance and most importantly the way he communicates with employees, sends out extremely powerful positive energy throughout the organization, setting off a virtuous cycle of individual and organizational greatness.

"What leadership boils down to, is people. Whatever your style, whatever your method, you need to believe in yourself, your ideas and your staff. Nobody can be successful alone and you cannot be a great leader without great people to lead. You have to walk the walk as well as talk the talk. Nobody respects a leader who doesn't know how to get his hands dirty and innovate personally. The trick is in striking the right balance between empowering your staff and being an example for them to follow", says the well known British business tycoon Sir Richard Branson, founder of U.K's Virgin Group[14]

Those who understand the value and power of connecting with people not only practice it themselves but also promote the same across the

---

[14] http://www.virgin.com/entrepreneur/richard-branson-how-be-real-leader

organizations they lead. No one could have demonstrated this in action more than Marissa Myer, president and CEO of 'Yahoo!'. When she broke the robotized culture that the industry had cultivated over the years by revoking the 'Work From Home' option in early 2013, she demonstrated that very insightful understanding about the power of human interaction and communication, which visionary leaders must possess.

Though, quite expectedly, her decision attracted a lot of criticism from all quarters, particularly from some of Yahoo's 11,500 employees, the message in an internal memo she sent out regarding this, was very clear. The memo - reportedly leaked out by irate employees - said "To become the absolute best place to work, communication and collaboration will be important, so we need to be working side-by-side...

That is why it is critical that we are all present in our offices".[15]

While critics virtually ranted and analysts set out making calculations about 'cost savings' and 'productivity', Marissa spoke about becoming 'the best place to work'. That's a huge - and brilliant - difference in perception between a strategic leader and operational managers. Including this transformation, she must have done a lot of things right, going by the outperformance of Yahoo's stock price, beating both Nasdaq as well as rival Google consistently since July 2012, the time she took charge. While Nasdaq moved from 2976 to 4052 (36%), and Google rose from $294 to $520 (77%), Yahoo clocked a gain of 113% rising from about $16 to nearly $34 between July 2012 and May 2014.[16]

---

[15] http://www.business-standard.com/article/management/marissa-is-wrong-113040700275_1.html

[16]

http://finance.yahoo.com/echarts?s=YHOO+Interactive#symbol=YHOO;range=2y

Insightful wisdom comes naturally to gifted people. Great philosophers and saints perhaps belong to this category. With others, it can be cultivated with conscious efforts, through observation and introspection, and over time it becomes second skin, reaching the scale of intuition.

Deep self awareness that comes from introspection of one's own strengths, weaknesses, mistakes and triumphs, gives us the ability to understand other people. It's very easy to succumb to subjective interpretations of human behavior based on our own psychological frame of reference. Those who have developed a higher self-awareness are capable of breaking through those subjective lenses and see the truth. It's like the difference between reading the temperature of water by dipping our fingers in it and measuring with a thermometer. If our fingers are cold the water feels warm, and vice-versa, but the instrument always tells us the right temperature. When human behavior is a complex phenomenon, how can one read another correctly, unless one of them has higher awareness and as a result, objectivity?

With higher awareness comes humility. The realization that we are all fallible humans, and also the realization that we all have the ability to grow to our full potential, provided that potential is systematically nurtured. That humility powers great leadership is not a new discovery in human psychology. It has always been the most essential trait in almost all leaders that history has seen, except psychopaths.

A recent (May 9, 2014) report published in 'The Times of India', talks about the writings of Lynda Gratton, professor of management practice, London Business School in her book, 'The Key'. In it she explains how authenticity - the 'inner journey' to understand and develop a sense of moral compass - and worldview, the 'outer journey', which is about understanding and being able to work across various stakeholders, makes a great leader.[17] The fact remains though, that this quality has always been important and was always present in every true leader of people. It's not that 'leadership qualities' per se is 'changing'. It's our understanding of what constitutes leadership qualities that has improved.

Not unlike a space vehicle, escaping from the gravitational pull that conventional conditioning has built over time, into a higher orbit of extraordinary success, requires the booster thrust of deep insightful thinking that drives you to the core of issues. The resultant ideas become powerful propellants which everyone wants to eventually adopt, even though initially, to preconditioned minds, these insights appear 'radical', 'revolutionary' or even downright 'quirky'.

---

[17] http://timesofindia.indiatimes.com/business/india-business/Humility-makes-CEOs-from-India-stand-out/articleshow/34848741.cms

The idea of 'Employees First, Customers Second' implemented by Vineet Nayar at HCL Technologies (HCLT) while he was the company's CEO, and also published as a book by the same name, raised nothing less than a storm worldwide, as the idea seemed to go against the well entrenched notion of 'customer is king'. It was labeled as 'turning a central idea taught at MBA programs on its head' to quote from an interview with Vineet Nayar published in Forbes (May 2012). His own response however, was a humble "I don't think it actually turns it on its head, it says the obvious".

"The trust between the management and the employees are amongst the lowest today in the world. The first thing that you need to do is create an environment of trust where the employees believe what you are saying and are willing to follow you wherever you are going. Therefore, by pushing the envelope of trust you can create an environment of trust,"[18] Vineet added further.

How did this philosophy influence HCL Technologies? The mini e-version of Vineet Nayar's book published by Harvard Business Press, says "When HCL Technologies embarked on the 'Employees First' journey in 2005, shifts in the IT services market had left the company struggling to compete with its global competitors. After a series of successful experiments that turned the management structure upside down and transformed the company, HCLT is now one of the fastest-growing IT service partners in the world"

"In three years' time HCLT grew at a CAGR of 24% and increased its market capitalization by 186%, doubled the number of $10 Mn, $20 Mn & $50 Mn customers and tripled the number of $100 Mn customers; HCLT's revenue per employee is

---

[18] http://www.forbes.com/sites/karlmoore/2012/05/14/employees-first-customers-second-why-it-really-works-in-the-market/

amongst the highest in the Indian IT industry today; HCLT was also featured as one of the most innovative and disruptive companies globally –

- Included in the first ever Executive Dream Team published by Fortune

- Emerged as the top ranking IT Services company in APAC, in Forbes Asia's 'Fab 50 List'

- Ranked by TPI in the Top 6 Global Service Providers by TCV across ALL 3 geographies (Americas, EMEA, APAC)"[19]

Howard Schultz, chairman and CEO of Starbucks thinks no different when it comes to putting employees first. "Our mission statement about treating people with respect and dignity is not just words but a creed we live by every day. You can't expect your employees to exceed the expectations of your customers if you don't exceed the employees' expectations of management. That's the contract." he says in an interview with 'Entrepreneur.com' a

---

well known business magazine published by Entrepreneur Media Inc., California.[20]

It's a wonder why human beings - intricate biological creations of nature, reduce to 'human resource' - like inanimate economic commodities - that entrepreneurs strive to 'control' to achieve pre-determined business goals? Only a small number of real leaders think differently and demonstrate sensitivity towards the 'biological human'. If that was not true, the General Manager (human resource) of Maruti Suzuki's plant in western part of India wouldn't have been brutally burnt to death in a mob violence committed by agitated workers in July 2012. Allegedly, the murder was a result of escalated industrial tensions, and the already agitated workers venting their fury when one of them was suspended. The worker was allegedly suspended for beating up an official in retaliation of the official's casteist remarks against the worker. Emotional intelligence,

---

self awareness and restraint couldn't have been better invoked than in this situation, both on the part of the management collectively, the deceased official, as well as the workers. Yet the human relations problem remained a industrial pseudo-war going by the reaction of the country's commerce and industries minister who described it as ".....one incident (that would not) shake industry's confidence", adding that the state government is capable of 'handling the situation' and 'protecting the industry and investments'. The tone of the statement makes one feel as if the workers are at war with the management and the management must take guard. The stock price of the company tanked 9% the same day as the occurrence of the horrid incident. Since then, the stock price might have recovered, but it's unlikely that bitter memories of the avoidable violent human conflict culminating in a gruesome death would have stopped haunting the psyche of the organization.[21]

---

[21] http://timesofindia.indiatimes.com/india/Marutis-Manesar-plant-

Strained human relations are not an accidental fall out of work place pressures alone. It's an attitudinal flaw that is deeply ingrained by faulty conditioning too. When a wage dispute at Toyota India's plant near Bangalore led to a temporary factory closure and friction between the management and employees in early 2014, the dean of academics at Xavier Labour Relations Institute (XLRI), one of India's premium B-Schools specializing in 'Human Resource and Industrial Relations Management' said "The holding capacity of workers has traditionally been low. And in this case too, workers seem to be softening," The Economics Times bureau described the situation saying "Experts believe that the workers' latest position suggests that the management holds the upper hand." These reactions were despite that fact that workers demonstrated flexibility in their approach by saying "We are open to discussions (over wages) and we think both sides can come to an amicable solution"[22]

Isn't a win-win approach the sin-qua-non of negotiations? Aren't B-Schools expected to incorporate this fundamental principle in their HR and IR education? Doesn't thinking in terms of 'upper-hand' and 'workers' softening' because of 'low holding power' make a unhealthy 'power struggle' out of what really is a 'negotiation' situation?

When the country's industrial laws have laid out rules for both parties to follow, there's no need to make employees who are dependent on the entrepreneur for their very livelihood, feel guilty for speaking out their demands or for entrepreneurs to attempt extracting any advantage out of their natural dominating position.

---

[22] http://articles.economictimes.indiatimes.com/2014-03-27/news/48630114_1_toyota-kirloskar-toyota-india-wage-dispute

The labour unrest situation at Ford India is yet another example of "fractured human communication exaggerated by economic and social conditions," as the head of People and Change, KPMG India was reported to have said according to news published by 'The Times of India' in its March 26, 2014 edition[23]. "Individual livelihoods are at risk. You have to appeal to emotion and intellect of the employees," he added. "There has to be communication and logic. Labour issues typically arise when there is no logic." The partner and India leader - People and Organisation at Ernst & Young, who said this, couldn't have been more correct.

Another dispute going on for nearly a year since early 2013 involving Bajaj Auto, one of India's leading manufacturers of two and three wheeler vehicles, projects a prominent example of how absence of communication and logic creates

---

[23] http://timesofindia.indiatimes.com/business/india-business/Companies-trip-up-on-skills-to-tackle-labour-unrest/articleshow/32698230.cms

avoidable industrial stress. While the management met the workers' demands half way, the workers were not satisfied, which led to a stalemate and the management acting tough. When pointed out by the Financial Express correspondent in an interview, that there is erosion of trust between the management and the workers according to Industrial Relations experts and that increasing this trust can resolve disputes, the company's Managing Director Rajiv Bajaj ridiculed the idea, calling it as mere armchair wisdom preached by academics that was far from reality, and that plant management was a 'contact sport' that required courage and not commentary.[24]

If the analogy of 'contact sport' implied something like 'wrestling', then it makes a 'raw power game' out of a 'subtle human relations' issue. The competitive advantage in any case is always completely loaded in favour of the management, whether economically,

---

[24] http://www.financialexpress.com/news/rajiv-bajaj-managing-a-plant-is-a-contact-sport-that-calls-for-courage/1244708/1

socially or psychologically. It's important to understand that workers in an organization are not out to overpower management - they cannot afford to in any case. They are well aware of their economic dependence on their jobs for fulfilling their aspirations and looking after their families. They are not a bunch of psychopaths who must be tamed in order to get work done. Their social-emotional-intellectual make up makes them vulnerable and prone to outbursts. Even white collared employees engaged in cerebral rather than physical work find it difficult to apply what modern management calls as 'Emotional Intelligence'. So why not give blue-collared workers the benefit of doubt?

Those who have read or heard about Nonviolent Communication (NVC), would understand the preceding argument. NVC was developed and evolved by Marshall Rosenberg, an American psychologist, beginning in the 1960s from his search for a way to promote peacemaking skills. It has been widely applied in organizational and business settings as well as other situations as diverse as parenting, education, mediation, psychotherapy, healthcare, addressing eating issues, prisons, and as a basis for a children's book, among others. Rosenberg has also used it in peace programs in conflict zones including Rwanda, Burundi, Nigeria, Malaysia, Indonesia, Sri Lanka, Colombia, Serbia, Croatia, Ireland, and the Middle East including the Occupied Palestinian Territories.

NVC works on the idea that all human beings are capable of compassion and only resort to behavior that harms others when they don't recognize more effective strategies for meeting their needs. Psychological conditioning through habits of thinking and speaking that lead to the use of violence (psychological and physical) are learned through culture. NVC attempts to de-condition deep seated violent traits, by helping people identify their own as well as the needs of others, the feelings that surround these needs, and through this awareness process, achieve harmony.[25]

Socio-economic conditions would always limit workers' 'holding capacity', to quote the term used by the dean of XLRI in the Toyota case. So would it be in the Bajaj Auto situation, with the management determined to deal with trouble makers firmly even if it means a six-month shut down. Both situations best represent an opportunity to apply 'Transactional Analysis', a theory of psychology and psychotherapy that integrates psychoanalytic, humanist and cognitive approaches, developed by the Canadian-born US psychiatrist Eric Berne in the late 1950s.[26]

It would be worth understanding what ego-states of the Parent-Adult-Child model fits the 'management' and the 'workers' or the nature of 'Transaction' between the 'management' and the 'experts', who are pooh-poohed as useless 'academics', and who

---

[25] http://en.wikipedia.org/wiki/Nonviolent_Communication
[26] http://en.wikipedia.org/wiki/Transactional_analysis

apparently live on a different planet, away from the practicalities of life!

In the ancient Indian epic 'Mahabharata', which is a great source of learning and inspiration for many a management guru, Lord Krishna himself never fought in the Kurukshetra war. His role was non-combatant, as merely the charioteer and advisor to Arjuna, one of the five 'Pandava' brothers warring against the huge army of their cousins and rivals, the 'Kauravas'. Yet, in the end only the 'Padavas' survive the war.[27] The war is symbolic of conflict of conscience with the demons in the mind, where listening to reason and intellect provides the direction.

Simply listening, understanding and empathizing, can build bonds far beyond 'matching industry standards of compensation'. No industry and no company is immune from economic ups and downs. It makes a

---

[27] http://en.wikipedia.org/wiki/Krishna_in_the_Mahabharata

huge difference whether you have a team of employees who identify with the company with pride, and work with passion in their hearts, or a bunch of unhappy factory workers executing pre-assigned tasks without complaining, because they need the job. This is more relevant when companies go through bad times. We have come a long way since the evolution of the modern industrialized world, and the hilarious depiction of its evils in 'Modern Times', a 1936 comedy film written and directed by the iconic Charlie Chaplin, haven't we?[28] It shows the tramp become almost a robot, repeatedly performing a given task mindlessly. So much so that the hand movements he makes for tightening bolts continues unconsciously even after his duty time.

It takes a lot more than sales and profit numbers to become a 'world class' organization, and as much time and effort to build 'employee equity' as the

---

[28] http://en.wikipedia.org/wiki/Modern_Times_(film)

huge investments companies make to build 'brand equity' with the customers.

Companies should spend more time and resources on teaching senior leadership how to lead than training followers how to follow. If that sounds like unwanted advice, ponder over this.

"Leadership remains the No. 1 talent issue facing organizations around the world, with 85% of companies in our survey rating it as "urgent" or "important." But only 14% of companies say they do an excellent job developing global leaders - the largest readiness gap in our survey", says the Global Human Capital Trends 2014 survey of 2500+ CEOs and HR leaders in 90+ countries carried out by Deloitte, the largest network of professional services and advisory firms in the world.[29]

---

[29] http://dupress.com/periodical/trends/global-human-capital-trends-2014/

Yet, perhaps more is written and more corporate training programs are conducted on the latter than the former. The assumption is that 'we know it all, you learn'. Take 'team-work' for example. This is probably the favorite topic for both trainers as well as managers who engage them. Of course every leader wants to 'have' a 'great team' working for him, and is perfectly justified to nurture that wish. No matter how much you oil the squeaking wheels of the 'operational band-wagons', without a great leader to pull the wagons along, can a great 'organizational team' exist? If leader-managers carry compartmentalized views of their own 'sales-team', 'finance-team' 'production-team' etc, it's like counting the trees - the functional teams - but missing the woods - the organizational team. A great leader must provide the power of a locomotive engine first, for the rest of the well lubed players to follow, rather than a 'I'm OK, You're not OK' attitude.

Forbes featured an article titled 'Five Ways to Become a Better Team Player', in its Mar 2012 issue[30]. The write up tells 'employees' in a typical business organization - because 'job requirements of today's employees have changed profoundly' - how they can become 'good team players' by following five tips that Harvard Business School professor Amy Edmondson writes about in a new book. In a nutshell, the five tips from the author are:

(i) Make continuous learning and action, the rule.

(ii) Ensure everyone participates.

(iii)Communicate all you know and do, don't assume others know.

(iv)Share information, analyze and decide scientifically.

(v) Don't fear failure, accept it as successful learning.

Now think of an organization where senior leadership is not sensitized or oriented towards

[30] http://www.forbes.com/sites/dorieclark/2012/03/28/five-ways-to-become-a-better-team-player/

practicing and promoting what the above 'behavior and attitude' ideas really boils down to, themselves - Learning, Involvement, Communication, Objectivity and Courage. Will great team-work ever happen in such organizations? Bad team players don't exist, only bad team leaders do.

The responsibility of correctly judging whether or not such an attitude is blocking both individual and organizational success lies somewhat paradoxically entirely upon the leader himself. It requires a great deal of moral strength, emotional maturity, humility, introspection and wisdom on the part of leaders to undergo any kind of 'psychological reengineering' themselves.

Organizations led by truly wise and enlightened leaders run like well oiled engines, their leaders providing the necessary lubrication for eliminating inevitable frictions arising from human differences - call it idiosyncrasies, eccentricities, biases, personality, weaknesses - whatever. When every company in the marketplace is sailing in the same ocean - the socio-economic environment, doesn't 'people-power' turn out to be the only differentiator that steers it towards dazzling success, an also-ran or an outright failure?

This is used by Hollywood divas! Trust me.

3

'Customer Care'?
Really?

Don't try to tell the customer what he wants. If you want to be smart, be smart in the shower. Then get out, go to work and serve the customer!

- Gene Buckley, Ex-CEO Sikorsky Aircraft

"Can you sell ice to an Eskimo? It might not be one of your action items here, but that's the kind of energy this department demands. (Among other things), your attention will also be taken up by activities like assisting customers who would like to cease their service, providing the most relevant retention offers - such as, but not limited to, promotional discounts - and planning upgrades and downgrades."

That was a recruitment advertisement for a 'collections and order management' position in one of India's top ranking listed company's BPO business.

"A pen that won't work or a melon hat for a cat. Maybe not like this but many more wacky products await you. All you need to do is use your gift of gab. If you can make us buy it, you can go home a winner."

That was a call for entries for a "A Minute to Think, A Minute to Sell" student event called 'Mad Ad' organized annually by the Student Activity Center of a well known Indian University. Through its 'literary society', the university itself "aims to provide a platform for the leaders of tomorrow to express their views"

It's difficult to miss the essence conveyed by the two messages shown above. Both are real life cases. One common thing both are clearly saying is that the ability to talk customers into buying makes you a hot-shot candidate - the industry seeks it and B-Schools teach it. If that's the orientation prospective business leaders are exposed to, then the road to successful business development has already hit a dead end.

Covering a brief review of two books on 'salesmanship', The Economist (Apr 2012) made the following concluding comments - "Being a salesman in the internet age is getting harder. Sales forces are being cut and replaced with technology, and the job is losing its appeal. The popularity of the title "sales associate" on LinkedIn, an online network, has fallen dramatically in the past four years. BMW's boss in America, Ludwig Willisch, admitted to the authors of the McKinsey book that it is hard to persuade people to go into sales these days. As......a former

Xerox salesman......said, "when you're in sales...it's lonely and it's a war."

The article was titled 'Ice to the Eskimos - Can the dubious art of selling become more scientific?'[1] Look up for the meaning of the word 'dubious' in the dictionary or on Google and you will see 'hesitating or doubting' and 'not to be relied upon; suspect'. The synonyms aren't any positive either.

How many 'sales persons' do you welcome with delight when they call upon you, either at your door, or on your telephone, or while in a store, no matter how pleasing, friendly or cheerful a disposition they put up? Why does the 'sales person' conjure an image so despicable that everyone wants to avoid the clan? The answer to this question is as clear as daylight from the words of Gene Buckley quoted at the beginning of this chapter. If students of business management are so conditioned that at the end of

---

[1] http://www.economist.com/node/21552189

the day, inducing the customer to buy makes them winners, and if business organizations also look for those very qualities which 'selling ice to an Eskimo' implies, then no salesperson would have a respectable place on this earth.

So, what's wrong with this conventional mantra of salesmanship? The short and crisp message "Make a customer, not a sale" from Katherine Barchetti, provides the answer. Ms. Barchetti was once a retail success story as a high-end fashion clothier in Pittsburgh, Pennsylvania (U.S.A), whose philosophy echoes that of many other illustrious business leaders who also crafted brilliant success stories for their organizations. Perhaps the power behind the otherwise brief message made it top the list of '40 Eye-Opening Customer Service Quotes' published in Forbes as recently as Mar 2014[2], as well as made 'Barchetti Shops' a leading case study which Tom Peters - well known as the author of the best seller

---

[2] http://www.forbes.com/sites/ekaterinawalter/2014/03/04/40-eye-opening-customer-service-quotes/

'In Search of Excellence' - uses in his customer service training video called 'Service with soul'[3]. The immensely strong imprint her company has left, long after it filed for bankruptcy in 1997 - allegedly due to theft and abuse of the store's customer service policies - speaks for itself. Her fall as a clothier surprised many, because at one point the upscale 'K Barchetti Shops' established in 1969, had charted extraordinary success with sales topping several hundred dollars above the national average. She was lauded for her tenacity, business savvy and aggressive customer service by Wall Street Journal in 1993.[4]

Selling is not about hypnotizing customers with glib talk; hypnotism doesn't last, genuineness does. Like the euphoric irrational boom that eventually gets knocked out by reason in stock markets, customers will sooner or later discover the truth. So nothing

---

[3] http://www.youtube.com/watch?v=OzV9ckz8TuE
[4]
http://www.bizjournals.com/pittsburgh/stories/1997/11/24/story4.html?page=all

less then building customer trust will work in the long run. Jack Welch, former CEO of General Electric and author said "If you don't have competitive advantage, don't compete". But the fact of the matter is that competitive advantage doesn't exist in the long run. The strongest proponent of this economic reality is Michael Porter who in his breakthrough work published 25 years ago, contended that over time competitive advantage was not sustainable.[5] Economic theory already tells us that in the long run only normal profits are available to all firms in competitive markets. This is more relevant to the likes of Fast Moving Consumer Goods (FMCG) industry, where differentiation is thin and technological entry-barriers are virtually absent. So, while you have to contend with normal profits in the long run, between now and the future, you have the opportunity to build 'trust'. You can't afford to outsmart customers now and expect them to prefer you in the long term.

---

[5] Michael Porter, Competitive Strategy (Free Press, 1980)

Unfortunately most managers are far too busy drawing, chasing and pushing short term sales targets, as well as incentivizing them, to realize that without first building the back-end genuineness, front-end sales people would only end up building distrust, or if the expression may be used - badwill.

It's like the huge stress gradually building up at fault-lines that eventually gives way, producing earthquakes. Leaving the customers with no choice but to buy your products should come not from shoving every other product out of sight, but from standing out as extra-ordinary from a plethora of ordinary. Yet, would any salesperson have the courage to be critical of the product he or she is supposed to 'sell'? Obviously not, for the fear of antagonizing the boss or risking his or her job! So what's the brouhaha about glorifying 'best sales performers' each quarter if the cookies are crumbling from within? In fact this is a perfect recipe for short-term gain and long-term pain, a perfect example of being 'penny-wise and pound foolish'. You can't be the best by fooling all the people all the time - because you just can't!

How does clocking 41 consecutive years of profitability, being the only profitable and solvent company in the industry for 23 consecutive years[6], while most of the industry's major players declared bankruptcy in the past 10 years[7] sound for an airline? Herb Kelleher, founder and former CEO of Southwest Airlines (U.S.A), sums up the airline's stupendous success in six words "quality service at a low price". Of course those are stereotyped goals which one would expect everyone to pursue, but what sets Southwest distinctly apart is the extremely cutting-edge belief that Kelleher practiced and preached in his company, revealed in his statement that followed after a brief pause "Then you infuse that with a spiritual attitude about people, and you

---

[6] http://www.youtube.com/watch?v=OzV9ckz8TuE
[7] http://www.businessinsider.com/case-study-how-southwest-stays-profitable-2012-6?IR=T

really get something that's unbeatable". That drives the point home as smoothly as hot knife through frozen butter.

The only holy grail of companies like Barchetti and Southwest Airlines is an obsession with caring for the customer. 'Customer Care' should come down from placards on the walls and spill all over the market place, and into customers' minds.

If salespersons are programmed into believing that selling is a 'war' and a 'lonely' one too - like the comment made by the salesman from nothing less than a multinational corporation such as Xerox - it sounds like a commando operative being left in a jungle all alone to fend for himself!

The absolute undiluted responsibility of putting the back-end of 'genuineness' in place and providing full support to 'front-end' sales people so that they don't feel 'lonely' rests on the CEO's shoulders. So does the responsibility of drawing up the description for front-end sales jobs which should read as 'We have a great product that fulfills customers needs. It's your job to correctly explain about it to customers. It's also your job to understand the reasons why some customers may not want to buy the product'. Leave the 'comparison with competitors' products' to the back-end. There's no point in salespersons bombarding the customer with 'my product is better than competition' rant, because customers are going to face the same monologue from rival salesmen too and make their own choice anyway. Whether customers rejoice or regret their decision later would depend on to what extent the product backs the claims made by glib sales talk! Better make sure they experience the former. 'Hard selling' may work for breaking 'block-buster' records or hitting the 'top-20' list for 'fleeting tastes' such as movies or music albums, not for drawing sustainable 'likes' from consumers. Yet, the fact remains that even with movies, music or with books, there are 'ever-green hits' and 'all-time classics'.

It's the back-end organization's job to get the competitive advantage in place and market it well, not the salesman's. Just as a single good intentioned political leader finds it hard to dismantle years of bad image built up by his party and to generate goodwill and trust from the electorate for his leadership capabilities, building customer goodwill becomes an uphill task if the foundation is weak. Punishing the 'underperforming' salesman or rewarding the 'smart' one, only becomes a counterproductive exercise.

In the battle for market supremacy, who are the victims? Rivals or consumers? Carpet bombing may destroy enemy territory - even competitors are in the warfare voluntarily, with full preparedness to battle it out in any case - but the real sitting ducks are gullible consumers! For the same reason, when the war gets nastily unscrupulous, rivals are also known to strike at each others' jugular vein, attempting to sabotage consumer goodwill bonds, believing and living by the maxim 'everything is fair in love and war'. Everyone has heard of weird things happening to products and services of companies that otherwise enjoy strong brand equity. Worms in chocolates and beverages, wired internet lines suddenly cut 'accidentally', surrogate slander of competitors' products through cleverly crafted advertisements and so on. Then the law has to struggle to resolve squabbles that arise, a huge loss of time and resources, while consumers are left more confused than ever.

It's one thing to have a great product or service and then provide honest and complete information to consumers, as to how they stand to be benefited by using it; and quite another to literally beguile them, regardless of the product or service quality! Bulk of the stupefying is done by deceptive advertisements.

There's a huge difference between the humorous exaggeration behind a tennis court being illuminated with brilliantly white teeth serving as floodlights - as in the case of the teeth-whitening chewing gum brand 'orbit', and the demonstration of hair strength by showing a model effortlessly dragging a truck with her hair - as in the Garnier Fructis Long and Strong shampoo ad. Human hair is strong enough to do that in any case. The Guardian (U.K), in an article titled 'Secrets of human hair unlocked at Natural History Museum in London' (27 May 2004), reported that "Hair is strong. A single strand could hold 100g (3oz) in weight: the combined hair of a whole head could support 12 tonnes, or the weight of two elephants."[8] Not when yanked from the scalp though, and certainly not because of the shampoo. The subconscious messages imprinted on the mind are different in the two advertisements.

---

[8] http://www.theguardian.com/uk/2004/may/27/sciencenews.research

One very prominent and successful 'Ad-Guru' and theatre personality is known to have said 'advertisements don't lie, they only exaggerate the truth'. Search for 'false advertising' in Wikipedia and you will see a whole compendium of various surreptitious methods used to mislead consumers. Even though false advertising is illegal in most countries, advertisers manage to clandestinely lure consumers in ways that are legal, or even if technically illegal, practically unenforceable.[9]

In order to curb the ill effects of misleading advertisements, most countries worldwide have regulatory frameworks in place, which also keeps responding to changing needs. The recent 'Truth In Advertising Act - 2014 (TIAA)' bill introduced in March 2014 in the U.S. Congress is a case in point. The bill asks the Federal Trade Commission (FTC) to develop a "regulatory framework" for ads that significantly change the people in them through

---

[9] http://en.wikipedia.org/wiki/False_advertising

image-altering techniques like "photoshop." Research shows that higher exposure to beauty and fashion magazines makes young girls more prone to developing a negative body image and eating disorders. This motivated a public interest group to push for and sponsor the bill. "Just as with cigarette ads in the past, fashion ads portray a twisted, ideal image for young women. And they're vulnerable. As sales go up, body image and confidence drops" a co-sponsor for the bill said.[10]

Companies and their marketing partners spend a lot of time and money to understand as well as to influence consumers' buying behavior. But just how much penetration into the consumers' mind stops short of coercion? 'Psychology Today', a leading magazine published by Sussex Publishers (U.S.A), explained in an Oct 2011 article how Steve Jobs knew what consumers wanted, more than what

---

[10] http://time.com/48853/lobbyists-push-congress-to-curb-misleading-photoshopped-ads/

consumers knew themselves.[11] Steve Jobs loathed 'Market Research'. Not because he disliked probing into people's minds, but because he believed it was useless. His reply to the question "how much market research was conducted to guide Apple in its incredible string of new product successes" was a curt "None. It isn't the consumers' job to know what they want" the article reported. "Get closer than ever to your customers. So close that you tell them what they need well before they realize it themselves", Steve Jobs was quoted by Forbes in its Mar 2014 issue.[12] Whew! No one would like to be snooped over the shoulders, would they? Especially if the information gathered is going to be used to induce them into some action - for example buying something. Well, Apple must not have actually snooped over its customers though - they used psychology, and Steve Jobs had the uncanny ability to anticipate what customers might want in future.

---

[11] http://www.psychologytoday.com/blog/inside-the-consumer-mind/201110/how-steve-jobs-knew-what-you-wanted
[12] http://www.forbes.com/sites/ekaterinawalter/2014/03/04/40-eye-opening-customer-service-quotes/

But whether it borders on unethically exploiting human weakness is controversial.

Despite extraordinary talent, it was not that Steve Jobs had an unblemished reputation. In a previous (Oct 2011) issue, Forbes describes Steve Jobs' management style in 'Five Dangerous Lessons to Learn From Steve Jobs', stating: a) not listening to your customers b) lack of transparency c) distorting reality to convince what is unbelievable d) micromanaging every detail e) abrasive, brutal approach towards people[13] - with a 'don't try this at home' warning. It literally describes Steve Jobs' extraordinary abilities as nothing less than that of a stunt artiste saying "But don't allow Steve Jobs' success to lure you into adopting (or accepting) his management style. That's the route to alienating co-workers and stoking workplace discontent, without delivering any of Steve Jobs' magical results."

---

[13] http://www.forbes.com/sites/chunkamui/2011/10/17/five-dangerous-lessons-to-learn-from-steve-jobs/

Nearly the same remarkable phenomenon was created by J. K. Rowling. Perhaps she wouldn't have been the runaway success that she is, had she not figured out what can catch the fancy of the millions who became voracious Harry Potter fans, ravenously lapping up one after another of her books in the series. Since the release of the first novel, 'Harry Potter and the Philosopher's Stone' in June 1997, her books became a huge commercial success worldwide. As of July 2013, sales of the Harry Potter series clocked between 400 and 450 million copies and had been translated into 73 languages. The last of the series reportedly sold around 11 million copies in the United States alone within the first twenty-four hours of its release.[14].

There's nothing wrong with making and selling digital devices, nor with being a step ahead of the consumers. No one would have imagined life without the traditional bank teller till the Automated

---

[14] http://en.wikipedia.org/wiki/Harry_Potter

Teller Machine (ATM) was invented. The worry comes from the adverse effects of digital addiction. Aren't smart phones and other digital devices not charting a cult-like following - feeding consumer fancy for experiencing digital thrill, just as J.K.Rowling's Harry Potter series found and fed the lure for fantasy in children? But addiction to reading 'fantacy' is not the same as addiction to gadgets. Professor Clifford Nass of Stanford Graduate School of Business did extensive research which showed that smart-phones adversely impact our stress levels and cognitive ability.[15]

For someone whose job is to successfully run a business that makes smart-phones and to keep its shareholders happy, this poses not only an ethical dilemma but also a sustainability challenge. Parents wouldn't mind their kids devouring Harry Potter, but it would be hard to find any parent who is not concerned with their kids' digital addiction.

---

[15] http://www.stanford.edu/group/knowledgebase/cgi-bin/2011/03/23/why-your-smart-phone-makes-you-dumb/

The damage is not limited to kids alone. The so called digital revolution has led even adults to unconsciously abandon rational thought. Dr.Vicki Panaccione known as 'The World's Expert in Parenting' and 'The Oprah Winfrey of Families', writes in 'parentingtodayskids.com', how experts and researchers are seriously concerned about 'information pollution', 'techno-brain burnout' and 'physiological addiction'. Some of the dangerous happenings that experts point out are:[16]

- the urge for constantly scanning our environment for something new, consciously or unconsciously, even when we are not in front of our computers, because we've trained ourselves to live in a perpetual state of distraction.

- technology has turned us into multi-taskers, even though research has found multitasking lowers efficiency about up to 50%!

---

[16] http://parentingtodayskids.com/article/smartphones-make-us-smarter-dumber/

- providing low quality sensory stimulation to our brain. Reading a paper book triggers a different part of the brain, with a high-quality form of stimuli, but an e-book on a Kindle, for example, offers low-quality stimulation!

- losing fundamental social skills, like reading subtle facial expressions during conversations.

What could happen when digital obsession gives way to greater consumer awareness? Would Apple (or any other firm in the smart-phone industry) have been what it is, had this techno-exhaustion taken place during the times of Steve Jobs? Would it be able to sustain itself if it happens now? Like the despicable sales person, would society soon loathe digital device makers? Research shows how these devices 'control' us and it won't be time before the new 'awareness' starts affecting the industry.

Have marketers and sellers, driven by the number chasing game, unabashedly been indulging in out-conning each other and out-smarting the consumer? Is 'competition', the hallmark of free enterprise and supposedly a boon for consumers, turning out to be a bane because of abuse of the freedom it grants to private enterprise? Are huge amounts of data gathered from and about consumers with the help of 'information technology' actually used to produce what consumers need and then genuinely educate and convince them with transparent information about product characteristics, or the same data is used as a 'weapon' in the hands of marketers to confuse the customer into believing the questionable to be the truth? Large companies operating in multiple markets worldwide spend a lot of resources to prevent their products from being impersonated by counterfeiters. Counterfeiters have no qualms about deceiving consumers. Ethics, to them, is as irrelevant as a USB cable is to a wireless device. But wouldn't the disguised deception perpetrated by the original producers themselves also classify as unethical practice?

Los Angeles Times reports in its 28 Oct 2012 edition, how the Federal Drug Administration warned Lancôme USA on the claims made in marketing for several of its anti-aging products, whose results matched with what might come from drugs, while the products did not go through the FDA vetting process to see if they can really produce the effects as claimed.

The same report also mentioned that in 2011, the 'National Advertising Division' of the 'Council of Better Business Bureaus' reprimanded a mascara ad starring Taylor Swift for showing her with digitally enhanced eyelashes and small-printing a disclaimer that her lashes were enhanced in post-production.

Procter & Gamble, which owns the product, subsequently withdrew the ad.[17]

Stephen King, former member of the Australian Competition and Consumer Commission and currently professor of Economics at Monash University writes in 'theconversation.com', one of Australia's largest independent news and commentary sites, that a print advertisement with a large statement designed to attract the reader, followed by smaller qualifying statements, clearly has an intent to mislead consumers. For those who don't notice the fine print, harm is done. He explains - based on a study of misleading 'snow reports' by private ski fields in the US as each resort tries to make itself look a bit better than the competition - that 'eventual' discovery of the truth by consumers takes time. Second, misleading advertising reflects dysfunctional market behavior. Businesses combat with each other to push the boundaries of

---

[17] http://www.latimes.com/features/image/la-ig-beauty-crackdown-20121028,0,4282901.story#axzz30Z8J4tmw

misleading marketing, even though they know that this upsets consumers in the longer term. Yet, they consciously choose to do it, for the fear of losing business in the short term.[18]

In another article, John Jewell, Director of Undergraduate Studies, School of Journalism, Media and Cultural Studies at Cardiff University says how clever advertising influences consumers' minds to 'buy' something that is available nearly 'free'. He explains how even though in the UK and in the US, public tap water is of outstanding quality, several brands of bottled water are making roaring business. At this rate, it won't be a surprise that in the next few years, bottled water will overtake carbonated soft drinks as the largest beverage category. In the UK alone, it's a £1.6 billion annual market. Britons drink more bottled water than fruit juices or wines and spirits. While advertisers use image building in their packaging and marketing - associating notions

---

[18] http://theconversation.com/where-should-we-draw-the-line-on-misleading-advertising-11730

of sophistication, health, youth, uniqueness, closeness to nature etc with bottled water and promoting it as a substitute for fizzy drinks - nearly 3m tons of plastic goes into its production worldwide, of which 80% ends up in landfills. The Pacific Ocean now has an area twice the size of Texas called the 'Great Pacific Garbage Patch' made up entirely of plastic deposits.[19]

Professor Stephen King rightly says "All legitimate businesses - as well as their customers - can gain by tighter advertising standards. It is only the charlatans who lose out".

The truth is that regulatory enforcements are like those ugly speed-breaker bumps - everyone driving down the road must encounter it, even though a simple 'pedestrian crossing' sign is enough to make a civilized person slow down instinctively.

---

[19] http://theconversation.com/bottled-water-is-the-marketing-trick-of-the-century-25842

What kind of businesses would better sustain in the long term, the ones who meticulously comply with every given set of guidelines, or those whose conduct sets the ethical benchmark for others to emulate, even in the absence of any regulation at all? Only civilized drivers are ultimately respected, aren't they? Whether in love, war or business, the word 'unfair' has only one meaning, no matter how much the camouflage is.

Just one more will make me the richest!

4

Help, the Goose
is Dying!

Business cannot succeed in societies that fail
- World Business Council for Sustainable
Development

Everyone's familiar with the Fortune Magazine's annual ranking of America's top 100 companies. Robert Levering and Milton Moskowitz had compiled the list for the magazine for the first time, and also brought out a book about the best practicing companies in the United States, analyzing how their excellent financial performance was the result of socially responsible conduct. The research done by Moskowitz challenged the historical assumptions regarding the financial effect of Environmental, Social and Corporate Governance (ESG) factors.[1]

The Center for Responsible Business at the Haas School of Business, University of California, Berkeley, instituted the 'Moskowitz Prize' in his honour, the only global award that recognizes outstanding quantitative research in socially responsible investing (SRI) and is presented at the annual SRI conference.

The 2013 Moskowitz Prize, conferred on Dr. Caroline Flammer, assistant professor at Ivey Business School at Western University (London, Ontario), is "one of the most important studies of CSR because it makes the strongest argument for a

---

[1]

http://en.wikipedia.org/wiki/Environmental,_social_and_corporate_gov ernance causal relationship between CSR and financial outcomes that has ever been made", said Lloyd Kurtz, faculty co-chair of the Moskowitz Prize. Analyzing more than 2,500 CSR proposals in publicly traded companies in the U.S between 1997 and 2012, Dr. Flammer found that long-term financial performance measured by return on assets, net profit margin and firm value significantly increased for companies that passed CSR resolutions (e.g., those which tackle environmental issues such as reduction of CO_2 emissions or social issues such as the implementation of non-discrimination policies). She also noted that implementing CSR leads to improved operating performance, happier employees and strengthened shareholder interest.[2]

Despite the fact that corporate leaders worldwide demonstrate greater awareness regarding the inseverable link between business and the socio-economic-environmental arena in which it operates,

_____

[2] http://www.triplepundit.com/2014/02/csr-financial-performance-linked-reveals-2013-moskowitz-prize-winning-scholar/

the biggest threat to human sustainability still remains in the grip of strong inertia. Even though many companies worldwide have already ingrained a culture of doing socially responsible business long ago voluntarily, India, a large and an attractive market for most of the world's big businesses, is the first country to integrate Corporate Social Responsibility (CSR) into its Company Law in 2013, making it mandatory for specified companies to spend a prescribed minimum amount out of their profits on CSR activities.

The reactions that emerged from various quarters of the industry as well as its partners to the mandatory CSR spend, makes one wonder whether the need and urgency of caring for the ecosystem has really sunk in. Leaving aside those who have already embraced CSR in its true spirit, what makes the rest nearly cringe at it, viewing it as a forced philanthropy? Is CSR and philanthropy the same thing?

The answer to this question probably lies in understanding the difference between constructing earthquake resistant buildings or providing disaster relief in the event of an earthquake, and actually 'stopping' an earthquake!

No, 'stopping' is not a misprint. 'Scientific American', a 168 year old magazine published in the United States, reports in its June 2010 issue that a thin layer of nano-clay gradually forms between cracks in a fault zone due to 'mineral-rich' water accumulating over time. This lubricates the tectonic plates enabling them to slide smoothly against each other. As the fault moves, new cracks are formed. But if enough lubrication is not formed in the new cracks, friction stress builds up between the plates now separated by the crack. Beyond a tolerance point, the pent-up stress gets suddenly released displacing the plates with a jerk, causing earthquakes. Scientists are experimenting whether by injecting some kind of lubricant in such cracks, it is possible to prevent, or at least reduce the intensity of earthquakes.[3]

This is not merely an analogy to illustrate the difference between 'prevention' and 'cure' in the context of corporate social responsibility. What appears as scientific findings about the occurrence of natural calamities, could actually open up the possibility that earthquake may not be completely natural at all and could be partly precipitated by human activity, if not in the near term, possibly over few hundred years. Why?

Is the 'mineral' in the 'mineral-rich' water that lubricates tectonic plates, same as what is extracted by the petroleum industry? Could a decrease in lubrication between the shifting tectonic plates be influenced by the oil and gas extraction process? If so, could the oil and gas industry be contributing to earthquakes? Chris Liner, a professor of petroleum

[3] http://www.scientificamerican.com/podcast/episode/auto-lube-keeps-parts-of-san-andrea-10-06-25/

seismology at the University of Houston explains in the Nov 2008 edition of 'Popular Science', another American magazine that has been published since 1872, that oil extraction is more like sucking with a straw from a sponge than from a pool of liquid. Petroleum deposits, naturally mixed with water and gas, lie between layers of porous rock. When the oil is extracted, water from the surrounding rocks flows into the void. It's like digging a hole at the beach and water from the surrounding sand flowing into it. And although some shifting of rock and deep sediment can occur, it wouldn't spur a major earthquake.[4]

Although that may sound comforting, but given that oil reserves world over are fast depleting, could it lead to the following situation in the long term? With depleted levels of lubricating stuff available to trickle down into fault lines - even if they are located much deeper than the deepest of oil wells - friction stress

---

[4] http://www.popsci.com/holly-otterbein/article/2008-11/what-fills-space-left-wells-when-oil-extracted-ground

between tectonic plates increases over time, raising the possibility and intensity of earthquakes. Of course this is only a layman's view. Only geologists and seismologists would know the truth.

The earthquake hypothesis could be only an exaggerated fear - hopefully - and be discarded as a figment of imagination unless someone proves it.

The real point in question here is whether 'sustainability' is being viewed in its right sense, far beyond a couple of generations following us. Correlate the damage to the ecosystem we are causing with the probable decline in human intelligence, and it compares with swimming against the tide where the currents grow stronger and swimmers, weaker. It is the responsibility of the living generation all the time, lest it turns into an irony. Like a child evolving into the 'future' - into adulthood, devoid of the subtle cultural and value learning that comes from healthy parental interaction, because parents were too busy provisioning for the child's 'future'! Can any amount of after-effort rectify the damage from years of negligence? If the goose that laid golden eggs also required to be fed some gold for its sustenance, the only way a steady supply of golden eggs could be obtained is ensuring the goose survives and not finding ways to boost egg production at the cost of neglecting the goose!

"When the winds blow, there are some who build walls and then there are others who build windmills". If the essence behind this Chinese proverb was to be interpreted as - the opportunist seeks to exploit even adversities, while the good Samaritan comes forward to protect, then several flourishing businesses could fall under the former.

What makes the multi-billion dollar bottled water industry thrive, when supporting the improvement of public water supply presents a socially responsible alternative? What makes pharmaceutical companies spend billions on curative research to fight disease, while several diseases arise due to poor hygiene and nutrition alone, that greater awareness, adequate food supply, preventive medicine and nutraceutical products can eradicate? Stepping in to boost social awareness and education for uplifting the quality of the country's citizens would do more good for its economy in the long run, than pestering political leadership for extracting business friendly policies, merely focused on expanding entrepreneurial profits, while the fabled trickle-down effect of capitalism remains a pipe-dream.

Retarded development in agricultural and allied sectors - irrigation, cold storage facilities etc - forcing farm labor into cities in search of factory jobs, where lack of industrial skills puts them in a weak bargaining position and forces them to settle for low wages, only creates a vicious cycle. While the industry may boast of 'low cost' advantage for catering to the export markets that benefits only the entrepreneur, the domestic economy suffers from poor aggregate demand because of the twin handicap of poor rural incomes and high urban cost of living for the migrated labor force.

How do we explain that even when the economy is sluggish, premium consumer durables - flat panel TVs, refrigerators, split air conditioners, smartphones - buck the trend in India? If this was true, as reported in Business Standard (Sept 2, 2013)[5], it only confirms an increase in income disparity because robust demand for premium goods couldn't have come from lower income segments who represent the majority in doldrums, of a 'perpetually emerging' economy. The phenomenon is not limited to consumer durables alone. Demand for premium consumer products is also rising. Take the example of cheese. The ₹12.5 billion (₹1,250 crore) Indian cheese market is expected to grow at 20% annually

---

[5] http://www.business-standard.com/article/companies/premium-durables-rise-in-preference-113090200036_1.html

says a report in The Economic Times (Sep 13, 2013)[6]. Who creates this higher demand for cheese? Leading pizza brands procure all their requirements from local sources. Besides this, direct consumption is also growing, not only for local cheese but global brands too. Obviously, those who can't have bread and milk have not taken to pizzas and cheese! If we believe in the trickle-down effect of sales and profit growth of premium goods, on the bottom of the economy, then there should be a corresponding increase in living conditions of the masses - food, health, education etc. But doesn't the humongous network of social service organizations called NGOs (Non-Governmental Organisations) take care of them? Critics would say so, which is like solidifying the soup because you can't eat it with a fork!

If every company registered in the country decides to fulfill its social responsibility by funding NGOs, what can we say about the end results? According to

---

[6] http://articles.economictimes.indiatimes.com/2013-09-13/news/42041654_1_cheese-business-parag-milk-foods-india-cheese

a report published in the Indian Express (Jul 7, 2010), the number of NGOs in India estimated by government agencies stood at 3.3 million (33 lakhs) as of 2009. This does not include NGOs registered under numerous acts other than the Societies and Public Trust Acts which were counted. A private organization set up to encourage transparency in the functioning of NGOs was reported to have said "....Nobody really knows the ground reality because this sector has grown very fast in the past many years. Besides, there have been no efforts to maintain an official database or even to encourage such entities to be transparent about their activities as well as funding."[7] Meanwhile, the number of active registered companies as on 31 May 2013 was 8.8 lakhs according to a report in The Economic Times (Jul 16, 2013).[8] That translates to roughly at least 4 NGOs per company assuming all companies - big and small - are accounted for. Given that

---

[7] http://archive.indianexpress.com/news/first-official-estimate-an-ngo-for-every-400-people-in-india/643302/0
[8] http://articles.economictimes.indiatimes.com/2013-07-16/news/40613264_1_annual-returns-1-5-lakh-registered-companies

mandatory spending on CSR activities is currently prescribed only for specified larger companies, and that the number of NGOs could be far more, as well as the lack of transparency in NGOs activities and funding, achieving the real goals of preserving and preventing degradation of society and environment would only be defeated and lost in murkiness.

More than funding NGOs engaged in various remedial activities, directly taking on the responsibility to reverse the erosion of the large rural sector would strengthen the entire economy in the long run due to its cascading effect. Only a strong domestic economy will eventually lead to a strong currency and a healthy socio-economic climate.

Social responsibility does not end with financial contributions to NGOs, though that is only one of the ways of discharging CSR. Do business enterprises practice socially responsible decision making? While cost-benefit analysis is rigorously professed and practiced throughout the value chain, is the social cost of every decision and action also taken into account?

Every socially irresponsible activity leaves behind a 'social cost' foot-print similar to carbon foot-prints caused by noxious emissions from various human activities. Growing concerns about carbon emissions have led to the measurement of carbon foot-print and to the development of internationally tradable carbon units called Certified Emission Reduction (CER) units on commodity exchanges.

Other initiatives have also been taken by governments worldwide for curbing environmental and social damage. Since fossil fuel powered thermal power plants emit large amounts of carbon dioxide into the atmosphere, in the recent past, energy efficiency rating labeled 'BEE Stars' was made mandatory in India for various manufactured appliances that consume electricity. A dedicated government agency, 'Bureau of Energy Efficiency' assigns the number of stars. More efficient appliances receive more stars, maximum being five. Most governments around the world have introduced laws to control the use of animals for testing consumer products. Legislations have also been put in place to prohibit child labor. Products of companies that rate lower on any of the above parameters face competitive disadvantage in international markets.

Even if all of the above has been accounted for, are we doing all that needs to be done in order to be non-exploitative towards all entities connected to business?

Early 2014 saw the creation of the 'Draft Modern Slavery Bill' in the United Kingdom, proposed to be placed before the parliament in June. The proposed law aims to end all forms of forced labour across the entire supply chain. The draft explicitly states in one of the paragraphs "the supply chains of major firms are extremely complex, involve many levels of outsourcing and subcontracting, and potentially an enormous number of companies. There is a danger that such complexity enables companies to absolve themselves of responsibility for how their goods are produced. As David Camp of the Association of Labour Providers told us, the "further you get away from the end user is where the murky stuff is". The effect is that some international companies that had factories in the ill-fated Rana Plaza building in Bangladesh may not even have known that they did. Wilful or unthinking blindness is no excuse."[9]

The death of nearly 1130 garment factory workers employed by international clothing brands and housed in the eight storey Rana Plaza building in Savar near Dhaka on April 24 2013, exposed the murky underbelly of cheap labor, low cost and high

---

[9]
http://www.publications.parliament.uk/pa/jt201314/jtselect/jtslavery/16 6/16608.htm

profit international fashion wear. The building was allegedly "declared unsafe, but the managers had quotas to meet" according to a follow-up report published in U.K's 'The Guardian', a year after the horrific accident.[10]

The gruesome killing of a general manager at Maruti Suzuki's plant in western India brought to surface the plight of casual and contract labor increasingly being employed by the industry to keep wage costs low. "There are many social security benefits that are not reaching workers...especially with the contractualisation of the workforce. In every industry, you will find a larger number of workers on contract than the regular workers...This has resulted in labor disputes and also resulted in labor violence," a senior official in the labor ministry reportedly said

---

[10] http://www.theguardian.com/world/2014/apr/19/rana-plaza-bangladesh-one-year-on

according to an article in The Economic Times on July 26, 2012[11].

On this count, what is immensely laudable is the message put up by Sir. Richard Branson on his group's website in bold letters "Let's end modern slavery", leading the movement with the group's policy not to engage in business with anyone "tainted by modern slavery", as well as exhorting other business leaders to "end this shameful scourge." He points out that according to experts, an estimated 20 million people are enslaved in making goods, many of which end up in global markets.[12] According to 'Walk Free', a global movement fighting to end the evil, the number is higher - nearly 30 million. The website of the organization that drives this movement 'www.walkfree.org' reports that modern slavery generates annual profits exceeding US $32 billion for slaveholders, quoting

---

[11] http://articles.economictimes.indiatimes.com/2012-07-26/news/32869493_1_contract-labour-labour-ministry-contract-workers
[12] http://www.virgin.com/richard-branson/let%E2%80%99s-end-modern-slavery

from International Labor Organization's (ILO) statistics.

If socially responsible conduct benefits all stakeholders involved in economic activity - as Dr. Caroline Flammer's research has proven - breaching the code not only denies those benefits but also loads the burden of social cost. That's a double blow. The converse is also true. Adopting socially responsible behavior not only leads to avoidance of the associated social cost but also bestows benefits. It's like flying an aircraft. Once you are in mid air, the only choices are either to keep the engines firing and move forward, or stop the engines and crash. There's no third option of hovering in one place, unless of course the aircraft is a chopper.

Consider the following cases and think about the negative social footprint each of it makes. These cases were reported by 'Business Standard' in its May 7, 2014 edition.[13]

A ship carrying phosphorus from Frankfurt to Mumbai caught fire in high seas in 1983. The ship was abandoned by the owner because the repair cost exceeded its insured value. The importer of the goods, Metal Powder Company, asked Oriental Insurance Company to pay compensation for non-delivery of the consignment according to the insurance contract. The insurer rejected the claim invoking a clause in the contract that the loss was due to the owner's insolvency because he had abandoned the ship, and the insurance did not cover losses arising from insolvency. The importer sued the insurance company and the trial court ordered payment of the claim with interest. The insurer appealed to the Madras High Court, which set aside the trial court's order and upheld the insurer's insolvency argument. The importer then appealed to

---

[13] http://www.business-standard.com/article/opinion/one-fire-doesn-t-lead-to-insolvency-114041300639_1.html

the Supreme Court which set aside the High Court verdict saying that merely abandoning the ship did not imply insolvency, because no court had declared the company as bankrupt. The verdict of the Supreme Court came after 30 years in April 2014.

In Purnya Kala Devi vs State of Assam, a motor vehicle hired by the government for public purpose met with an accident which caused a person's death. When the dependants of the deceased claimed compensation from the state government, it refused to pay, shifting the blame on the owner of the vehicle. When the dispute went to the Gauhati High Court, the court ordered that either the registered owner, or the insurer or the driver were liable to pay and not the government. The dependants appealed to the Supreme Court which pointed out that the definition of 'owner' in the Motor Vehicles Act included a person "in possession of the vehicle either under an agreement of lease, hypothecation or hire purchase." Therefore the government was liable to compensate the dependants.

In Indus Airways Ltd vs Magnum Aviation Ltd, the former issued post-dated cheques to the latter as advance payment towards future orders for spare parts. Later the deal was cancelled and Indus stopped payment for the cheque. Magnum filed a criminal case for dishonor of cheque under the Negotiable Instruments Act, and the dispute eventually went to the Delhi High Court which ruled that the post-dated cheques were issued against a liability therefore Indus is bound to honor it. An appeal was made to the Supreme Court, which quashed the High Court judgment, stating that no liability existed at the time of issuing the cheque since the purchase orders were never placed.

An Indian company ordered sugar from a Swiss firm. Disputes arose, which were referred to an arbitration tribunal constituted by the Refined Sugar

Association, London. When the award went against the Indian firm, it challenged it an Indian High Court. The court stated that it had no jurisdiction in the matter. The firm then appealed to the Supreme Court which pointed out that the terms of the contract clearly referred to the London association for resolution of disputes therefore the Indian company's appeal cannot be accepted in any Indian court.

A Jharkhand based company which manufactured glass and glassware made of opal glass was asked to pay higher tax on its inter-state sales of 'Glassware'. The company claimed a lower rate referring to a state government notification in which certain types of glass were eligible for lower tax, but the claim was rejected. The company petitioned the High Court which ruled in its favor. The government appealed to the Supreme Court against the high-court verdict. The Supreme Court, after referring to various dictionaries to discover the meaning of different

117

varieties of glass, upheld the demand of the revenue authorities, stating that 'Glassware' are generally ornamental products made from glass, and cannot be considered as a 'type of glass' that was eligible for lower duty under the said notification.

What a colossal loss of time, energy and resources of the country's judiciary, all the way from lower courts to the Supreme Court! Is the country's highest seat of justice expected to sort out petty squabbles? The total number of pending cases in twenty one Indian High Courts as of December 1, 2013 exceeded a mind boggling 4.43 million (44.34 lakhs) and the corresponding number in the Supreme Court was 65,661.[14] How does one expect the judiciary to function efficiently if every bickering is placed before a court? None of the above cases even warranted involving any adjudicating authority at all, leave aside the Supreme Court. It's like using a canon to kill a fly. If only the disputing parties

---

[14] http://zeenews.india.com/news/nation/65-661-cases-pending-in-supreme-court_897773.html

invoked their sense of fairness, common sense and logic, all of the above cases were as clear as crystal. Does this mindless frivolous litigation not put a huge social cost burden on society? These are only indicative examples. Be it industrial disputes involving managements and employees, consumer disputes involving products and services sold by companies, disputes between companies and regulatory agencies or between two business organizations, every single act of mindless litigation should also count as breach of social responsibility, because it puts a burden on society. The cost of maintaining law and order and dispensing justice eventually falls on the exchequer, and therefore on the tax payer, not to mention the indirect cost of enormous time and energy lost, and agony faced by litigants as well as other stakeholders involved. Every socially irresponsible decision leaves behind an adverse social footprint.

One can understand genuine mistakes made by companies, but when inadvertent loopholes in the letter of law that leads to deviation from its spirit are intentionally exploited for selfish benefits, it becomes impossible for the statute to blame the beneficiary for the mistake committed by the judiciary. All that can be done is to correct the letter of law prospectively or issue a clarifying notification to bring out its true spirit. Meanwhile, the beneficiary may already have gained an unfair advantage. If this practice becomes habitual, it could eventually spin a web of greed causing damage to all stakeholders including the culprit company.

Take the recent case of Ranbaxy Laboratories being acquired by Sun Pharmaceuticals from Daiichi-Sankyo in April 2014. The acquisition was priced at $3.2 billion, while Daiichi-Sankyo had paid $4.2 billion in 2008 for buying out Ranbaxy from its previous owners. The massive loss of value was primarily because of Ranbaxy's repeated non-compliance issues related to its manufacturing and quality in the US, the largest pharmaceutical market, which Daiichi was not able to resolve.[15] Think about the social cost of the cat and mouse game between Ranbaxy and the US patent authorities, and its ultimate victims, Daiichi Sankyo's shareholders.

Repeated violation of quality standards has also been the bone of contention behind regular rejection of perishable products exported to developed countries from India. Among other commodities, the ban on what is considered as the king of fruits, Alphonso mangoes caused the most distress to many a gourmand worldwide. So much so that 'The Guardian' described the recent ban in April 2014 as: "...(it) has left connoisseurs practically in mourning for an annual ritual that heralds the start of summer..."[16] The reason for the European Union ban until December 2015 was 'fruit-fly' infestation.

[15] http://www.business-standard.com/article/companies/sun-pharma-buys-ranbaxy-from-japan-s-daiichi-114040700737_1.html
[16] http://www.theguardian.com/lifeandstyle/2014/may/02/eu-mangoes-ban-indian-summer

Even though mangoes are also grown in other parts of the world, Indian varieties are considered to be the best. While the Indian government has demanded that the EU lift the ban, arguing that measures have now been put in place to address its concerns, the fact remains that this is not the first time. Indian commodities have faced quality issues from importing countries even in the past. It was only a year ago that a similar ban for the same reason was imposed by the US, along with other farm products for disparate reasons. Indian basmati was found to contain traces of a fungicide, tricyclazole, pomegranates and grapes were allowed only after pest risk analysis data was provided, litchis were not allowed due to a two year old issue of presence of excess sulphur dioxide.[17]

Incidents like these put governments in an awkward position defending the country's reputation and diplomatic relationships with other countries, while

---

[17] http://timesofindia.indiatimes.com/business/india-business/Indias-farm-products-face-US-import-hurdles/articleshow/21029622.cms

industry cries foul that quality issues are either being overdone with an ulterior motive or whines about the 'high cost' of various sanitation procedures.

While international trade and diplomacy expend energies on protecting each other's turf, nature follows its own course, adding to the distress and further motivating to win the tug-of-war game while the turf underneath is bruised beyond repair. Erratic weather and rapid deforestation have resulted in a 30% drop in the Alphonso mango crop in 2014, says a news report in The Times of India (May 11, 2014).

The disastrous effects of climate change are not restricted only to exotic crops that need specific weather conditions. A briefing paper titled 'Hot and Hungry: How to stop climate change derailing the fight against hunger' released by Oxfam International in March 2014, "analyses ten key factors that will have an increasingly important influence on countries' ability to feed their people in a warming world. Across all ten areas, serious gaps between what governments are doing and what they need to do to protect our food systems have been found. The results also show that while many countries – both rich and poor – are unprepared for the impact of climate change on food security, it is the world's poorest and most food insecure among them that are least prepared and most at risk."

Winnie Byanyima, Executive Director of Oxfam International presses the panic button hard saying "If governments act on climate change, it will still be possible to eradicate hunger in the next decade and ensure our children and grandchildren have enough to eat in the second half of the century." The positive tone in her words only subdues a warning that if governments don't act, even our immediate next generation will suffer.[18]

---

[18] http://www.oxfam.org/en/grow/pressroom/pressrelease/2014-03-25/world-woefully-unprepared-impacts-climate-food

Adding to the damage due to climate change is the huge amount of food wasted. A report published by the United Nations in Sept 2013 says that one-third of the world's food amounting to some 1.3 billion tonnes is wasted each year. This translates into annual economic losses of $750 billion and significant damage to the environment.[19] Can this loss not be prevented if private enterprise initiates the right actions, either on their own or in collaboration with governments? Farming co-operatives, food storage and distribution, agricultural research, farmers training etc are the areas where public-private participation could strengthen food security.

Would you ride a roller coaster or fly an aircraft if the quality of workmanship made it unsafe? It's no different when it comes to automobiles. Building trust in a brand takes years, but a single instance of negligence can destroy it. Auto makers do a lot to

---

[19] http://www.business-standard.com/article/news-ians/one-third-of-world-s-food-wasted-annually-un-113091201213_1.html

ensure the vehicles they make are completely road worthy. Despite stringent quality and safety checks, genuine manufacturing errors may arise, and if such defects are noticed in already sold vehicles almost every manufacturer has a product recall policy. Yet, like other unreasoned and unscrupulous human behavior, breach of trust does take place, which puts not only consumers at risk but also damages the painstakingly developed reputations of even internationally established names as well as leaves their governments red-faced. Once customers discover they have been cheated, it becomes an uphill task for them to really identify the culprits and - even if the real culprits are outside the company - getting customers to believe the company's innocence.

One of the largest, and perhaps the messiest of alleged 'corporate fraud' that 2013 saw - as some sections of the media labeled it - was a recall of 114 thousand 'Chevrolet Tavera' models manufactured by General Motors India between 2005 and 2013. The company's engineers in India had allegedly manipulated the engines to dodge emission standards and other regulatory specifications. This led to the dismissal of several senior employees for 'violations of company policy.'[20] Was it worthwhile for those responsible, to compromise on specified standards, only to report impressive sales performance or operating profits by evading excessive cost of rejections that honesty would have otherwise resulted in? Now that the fraud stands exposed, the long term slur on the company's reputation turns out to be far greater than the few millions attempted to be saved.

Even as children's nutrition supplement brands fight amongst each other for a greater share of consumers' wallets, the growing concern about junk food being pushed down the minds and throats of gullible children has recently raised a major uproar

[20] http://m.financialexpress.com/news/general-motors-fires-several-employees-in-india-us-after-probe-into-tavera-recall/1147504/

against multinational food giants in India. In response to a case filed by a non-governmental organization in 2010 in Delhi High Court, a committee was set up in 2013 to frame guidelines for food, as the "ill effects of eating junk food have been documented by public health experts and also pediatricians". After initial failed attempts by the food industry representatives to block the setting up of the committee itself, and their tactics to shift the blame on lack of physical activity, the working group identified 'packaged fried food' such as chips, carbonated beverages, instant noodles and confectionery as 'junk food' and also recommended strongly against celebrity endorsements for such food. Now the report is with the high court and awaiting a decision.[21] Will the food companies take an ethical path and do what is right or grumble about the profit impact and disregard social damage?

---

[21] http://www.business-standard.com/article/opinion/sunita-narain-junk-games-and-schoolchildren-114042700693_1.html

The 'R' in CSR needs serious introspection. 'Responsibility' being viewed as 'Philanthropy' is grossly wrong. Responsibility is an onus, while philanthropy is a gratuitous act. The recent 'Handbook on Corporate Social Responsibility in India' published by the international audit and consulting firm PricewaterhouseCoopers (PwC)[22] attempts to drive home this point. While referring to the various definitions of CSR by international agencies like the European Commission (EC), the World Business Council for Sustainable Development (WBCSD) and the United Nations Industrial Development Organization (UNIDO), the PwC document rightly points out that CSR and sustainability are inseparable saying that rather than focusing on what is done with profits 'after' they are made, sustainability driven CSR is about 'how' profits are made.

---

[22]
http://www.pwc.in/en_IN/in/assets/pdfs/publications/2013/handbook-on-corporate-social-responsibility-in-india.pdf

In fact none of the definitions given by the above bodies use the term 'philanthropy' or 'charity'. On the contrary UNIDO cautions by emphasizing "......it is important to draw a distinction between CSR - which can be a strategic business management concept - and charity, sponsorships or philanthropy. Even though the latter can also make a valuable contribution to poverty reduction, will directly enhance the reputation of a company and strengthen its brand, the concept of CSR clearly goes beyond that."

Human psyche has been so deeply hard-wired with the idea of 'laissez faire' that once capitalism was adopted as a system, it quickly led to be considered a 'birthright' and the notion set in that everything else was 'interference'. The 'trickle-down' effect which capitalism was believed to automatically bestow and thereby cause social development by default, never happened as originally intended. The core questions entrepreneurs need to ask themselves are 'Does this planet and its inhabitants exist because of us, or do we exist because of them?' and also 'Why has society allowed us to own economic resources and to produce goods and services that fulfill its needs, when the same could have been done by the society on its own as in communism or by governments as in socialism?'.

Left to itself, nature follows its own cycle to stay in harmony. Disrupting the cycle will eventually lead only to disaster. Consider the water cycle for example. Imagine a hypothetical situation wherein inhabitants of another planet suck out water from the earth's water bodies, then supply the same water to us in small packets as and when needed, in enough quantities to barely keep us alive. Would we earthlings be in any position to bargain for more if we were asked to either-take-it-or-leave-it, and the aliens defended themselves pointing to compliance with some inter-galactic minimum water supply act? What would earthlings do? Kill each other to reduce the number of mouths to feed? Would it be good enough for us if the aliens, in an act of philanthropy, took care of us if we were hurt or fell sick, and punished those who indulged in violence and murder?

Extending the above analogy, isn't unequal distribution of wealth and human development the evidence of a disrupted economic cycle and the root cause of social evils? The PwC handbook on CSR says "(While India) has grown to be one of the largest economies in the world, and an increasingly important player in the emerging global order, on the other hand, it is still home to the largest number of people living in absolute poverty (even if the proportion of poor people has decreased) and the largest number of undernourished children. What emerges is a picture of uneven distribution of the benefits of growth which many believe, is the root cause of social unrest. Companies too have been the target of those perturbed by this uneven development and as a result, their contributions to society are under severe scrutiny". Even though the resultant 'social unrest' couldn't have been more emphatically pointed out, the fact that 'abuse of Capitalism' is at the epicenter of the malady gets grossly diluted by the statement that follows. Companies must take on the 'Social Responsibility' for undoing the ills that abuse of capitalism has caused, and not feign to be victims of its effect.

Oxfam International, a confederation of 17 organizations spread over more than 90 countries, with its secretariat based in the U.K, works to influence international action towards reducing poverty and injustice. It was formed in 1995 by a group of independent non-governmental organizations and derives its name from the Oxford Committee for Famine Relief, founded in Britain in 1942. The body warns in a report published on 20 January 2014 that in a world of 7.04 billion people[23],

---

[23] http://wdi.worldbank.org/table/2.1

"wealthy elites have co-opted political power to rig the rules of the economic game, undermining democracy and creating a world where the 85 richest people own the wealth of half of the world's population". It makes an appeal to governments "to tackle inequality by cracking down on financial secrecy and tax dodging, including through the G20; investing in universal education and healthcare; and agreeing a global goal to end extreme inequality in every country as part of the post 2015 negotiations."[24]

"Globalisation makes it clear that social responsibility is required not only of governments, but of companies and individuals. All sources must interact in order to reach the Millennium Development Goals" Anna Lindh, the Swedish political leader who strongly advocated respect for international law and human rights once aptly said.

---

[24] http://www.oxfam.org/en/pressroom/pressrelease/2014-01-20/rigged-rules-mean-economic-growth-increasingly-winner-takes-all-for-rich-elites?utm_source=oxf.am&utm_medium=wMY&utm_content=redirect

Would it be possible to truly achieve the Millennium Development Goals (MDG), an ambitious mission the United Nations and its partners have set for a better world, with philanthropy alone? Among the eight specific goals[25] set to be achieved by 2015, the one that needs urgent attention is ensuring environmental sustainability.

The Secretary-General of United Nations Ban Ki-moon emphasized the urgency of the climate change problem in his opening remarks at a high-level meeting in Abu Dhabi in May 2014, intended to generate momentum ahead of the UN Climate Summit later in the year in New York. "Climate change is the defining issue of our time. If we do not take urgent action, all our plans for increased global prosperity and security will be undone"[26] he said. He also says in a report titled '2015 and Beyond: Perspectives on Global Development', published by

---

[25] http://www.un.org/millenniumgoals/
[26] http://www.firstpost.com/world/tackle-climate-change-before-its-too-late-ban-ki-moon-1508489.html

the United Nations, "Crafting a post-2015 development agenda presents an opportunity to build on the strengths of the MDGs and address challenges that have since emerged or were overlooked. Sustainable development with its three interconnected - economic, social and environmental - dimensions will provide the conceptual framework. To achieve results, we need the broad engagement of civil society around the world. The World Federation of United Nations Associations and UN Associations around the world have been critical to raising awareness about the MDGs and mobilizing action. As we look beyond 2015, this leadership and strong voice will be even more essential to realize our vision. I count on their continued advocacy and example in this effort. Let us work together to create a just world where all people live with dignity and hope."[27]

---

[27]

http://www.wfuna.org/sites/default/files/wysiwyg/images/acronym_5_3_text_lr.pdf

The Indian Companies Act 2013, section 135 (3) stipulates the setting up of a CSR committee within companies' boards. The role of the committee would be to formulate and recommend a CSR policy which shall indicate the activities to be undertaken by the company as specified in Schedule VII of the act. The schedule itself lists the following as CSR activities[28]

1. Eradicating hunger, poverty and malnutrition, promoting preventive health care and sanitation and making available safe drinking water.

2. Promoting education, including special education and employment enhancing vocation skills especially among children, women, elderly, and the differently abled and livelihood enhancement projects.

3. Promoting gender equality, empowering women, setting up homes and hostels for women and

---

[28] http://www.mca.gov.in/Ministry/pdf/CompaniesActNotification3_2014.pdf

orphans; setting up old age homes, day care centers and such other facilities for senior citizens and measures for reducing inequalities faced by socially and economically backward groups.

4. Ensuring environmental sustainability, ecological balance, protection of flora and fauna, animal welfare, agro-forestry, conservation of natural resources and maintaining quality of soil, air and water.

5. Protection of national heritage, art and culture including restoration of buildings and sites of historical importance and works of art; setting up public libraries; promotion and development of traditional arts and handicrafts.

6. Measures for the benefit of armed forces veterans, war widows and their dependents.

7. Training to promote rural sports, nationally recognized sports, Paralympic sports and Olympic sports.

8. Contribution to the Prime Minister's National Relief Fund or any other fund set up by the Central Government for socio-economic development and relief and welfare of the Scheduled Castes, the Scheduled Tribes, other backward classes, minorities and women.

9. Contributions or funds provided to technology incubators located within academic institutions which are approved by the Central Government.

10. Rural development projects.

Despite the steps being taken by governments and industry, what remains to be seen is whether the realization of real responsibility has sunk-in deep enough to be integrated into 'how business is done, or remains restricted to 'compliance' with selected few activities from among the choices given, by 'spending' the specified amounts towards NGO funding.

On this point, an interesting case is one of the demands made by the employees of Bajaj Auto. They wanted the company to allocate its CSR funds for their children's education. While section 135(5) of the Companies Act says that companies must give preference to the local area and areas around it where it operates, for spending CSR funds, the company has not yet accepted any of the employees' demands that include other issues.[29] Will the management accept this one demand even if it justifies refusing the rest and thereby gain from the goodwill leverage?

29

http://economictimes.indiatimes.com/industry/auto/automobiles/bajaj-auto-union-firm-on-demands/articleshow/33920617.cms

Paul Polman, CEO of Unilever spoke from his heart, pointing out precisely where the shoe hurts, the need to act urgently now, how his company transformed its mindset and what business leaders should do, in an extremely frank, soul searching, and emphatic interview published in McKinsey Quarterly (May 2014)[30]. Every statement that he made is so important and relevant for sustainability that it's impossible to compress it in a small paragraph here. Here is the briefest possible edited version of what he said.

"Capitalism....has come at an enormous cost: unsustainable levels of public and private debt, excessive consumerism, and, frankly, too many people who are left behind"

"Further development and population growth will put a lot more pressure on our planet."

---

[30]
http://www.mckinsey.com/Insights/Sustainability/Business_society_and _the_future_of_capitalism?cid=other-eml-alt-mkq-mck-oth-1405

"Capitalism needs to evolve, and that requires different types of leaders from what we've had before."

"Business is here to serve society. We need to find a way to do so in a sustainable and more equitable way...with resources...(and)....with business models.... and generate reasonable returns. (Problems like) small-hold farming, food security, and deforestation...require ten-year plans to address. But if.....you don't tackle these issues, you'll end up not being in business....Business simply can't be a bystander in a system that gives it life in the first place. We have to take responsibility..."

"We created the Unilever Sustainable Living Plan...(along with doubling turnover) we will reduce our absolute environmental impact, and increase our positive social impact. Because (this requires) a longer-term model..... I decided we wouldn't give guidance...and stop full reporting on a quarterly basis...to remove the temptation to work only toward the next set of numbers...alter the compensation system to (include) incentives related to the long term...(Due to stopping guidance) our share price went down 8% but that didn't bother me...the longer term....true performance would be reflected in the share price anyway"

"Thinking in the long term has (caused) strong success......over the past five years. Better decisions are being made....a more mature dialogue (is happening with shareholders)...about....strategic actions (that) serve long term interests, versus explaining short-term movements."

"That's very motivational for our employees. We may not pay the same salaries as the financial sector, but our employee engagement and motivation have gone up enormously over the past four or five years. People are proud to work on something where they actually make a difference in life, and that is obviously the hallmark of a purpose-driven business model. We're getting more energy out of the organization, and that willingness to go the extra mile often makes the difference between a good company and a great one."

"(long term thinking involves) delivering proof every year that we're making progress, (targets) often require investments for one or two years before you see any return. For instance,....creating new jobs for 500,000 additional small farmers, moving to sustainable sourcing, reaching millions......to improve their health and well-being. All of this is hardwired to our brands and all our growth drivers."

"It's not only corporate leaders who need to take a longer-term view of capitalism. Pension funds....believe in that mission (long term returns), but many of them.....might offer quarterly incentives to their fund managers, employ short-term hedge funds and others, disturbing the normal economic process......this activity actually destroys more value than it builds."

"In the coming 15 years, we need to align on the new Millennium Development Goals (set by the UN)"

"(If) more initiatives (are) undertaken by....... businesses to protect their long-term interests and the long-term interests of society, Governments will join these initiatives if they see business committed. It is......difficult for governments......as long as we don't adjust our outdated governance model."

"The Tropical Forest Alliance[31] is a good example of what can be done. If....deforestation, which accounts for 15 percent of global warming (continues), our business model and, frankly, our whole society are at

---

[31] A public–private partnership created by the US government and The Consumer Goods Forum to decrease tropical deforestation undertaken to source commodities, such as palm oil and soy. The alliance now consists of multiple nongovernmental organizations and national governments, including those of the Netherlands, Norway, and the United Kingdom.

risk. On top of that, the consumer is saying, "I'm not going to buy products anymore created through deforestation." So industry got together and said...."By 2020, we're not going to sell any more products from illegal deforestation, whether soy, beef, pulp, paper, or palm oil," that sent an enormous signal across the total value chain and generated action on the supplier side. Governments are now joining"

Even as business leaders like Sir. Richard Branson and Paul Polman demonstrate in thought and action, tremendous awareness and commitment towards doing socially responsible business, there's still a lot of catching up to be done by many others, before it becomes a positive contagion. How many companies have their strategic missions tied to the Millennium Development Goals? We still see private industry leaving no stone unturned to blame governments for interference in laissez-faire on many occasions and lobbying hard with their governments for 'business-friendly' policies, while conveniently forgetting that freedom comes with responsibility. Even seasoned private entrepreneurs have been heard openly protesting against the mandatory CSR spending rule introduced in the Indian Company Law saying philanthropy cannot be forced upon. As if the grudge coming from entrepreneurs in private industry was not enough, experts from international advisory firms also join in the whine. For example, one partner of Deloitte Haskins & Sells was quoted by the media complaining about CSR expenditure not being tax-deductible, and how that would "only impediment the voluntary spend by businesses, and will also lead to dissatisfaction amongst companies"[32]

'Responsibility' and 'Philanthropy' are two different things. How does one expect a parent to react, if a child views the need for 'good behavior' as 'imposed discipline' and asks 'what incentive will I get in

---

[32] http://www.business-standard.com/article/opinion/five-points-that-spook-india-inc-114041300641_1.html

return?' How would one explain to the child that good conduct was in his/her own interests?

There's an old prayer that goes "God grant me the serenity to accept the things I cannot change, courage to change the things I can change, and wisdom to know the difference." The relevance of this cannot be overemphasized in the contemporary world. CNN published in its September 27, 2013 edition,[33] the grim reality pointed out by scientists in the United Nations Climate Change Report, saying "Human activity has caused at least half of climate change in the last half-century, hundreds of scientists say. They are 95% certain of this, the surest they've ever been...(Activities such as) driving cars, running power plants on coal and oil, torching swathes of forestland and debris; anything involving burning carbon-based fuels and emitting greenhouse gases, (lead to) extreme weather patterns, particularly drought and flood, and they will probably get worse

---

[33] http://edition.cnn.com/2013/09/27/world/climate-change-report/index.html#!

this century." The report added the words of U.S. Secretary of State John Kerry in an official statement "Those who deny the science or choose excuses over action are playing with fire"

Interestingly, as part of the Kyoto Protocol many developed countries have agreed to legally binding limitations/reductions in their emissions of greenhouse gases in two phases. The first commitment period applies to emissions between 2008 and 2012, and the second, to emissions between 2013 and 2020. Between December 1997, when representatives of over 150 nations first met in Kyoto, Japan and December 2012, when the Kyoto Protocol extended to 2020 during a conference in Doha, Qatar, the target of cutting emissions to 5% below 1990 levels in the first phase remains underachieved to say the least, and embroiled in political bickering, divided opinions and denials. As the game of scrambling for credits but scampering from responsibility goes on, the ecosystem continues to be ruined. CBC News-Canada, in a scathing criticism published on Dec 31, 2012 with a title 'Kyoto climate change treaty sputters to a sorry end' said "The controversial and ineffective Kyoto Protocol's first stage comes to an end today, leaving the world with 58 per cent more greenhouse gases than in 1990, as opposed to the five per cent reduction its signatories sought."[34]

The irony of proven technological prowess failing to quell the impending climate change tsunami stands out like the foul smelling corpse flower tarnishing the rest of the otherwise fragrant botanical species. In one of the articles posted on the World Economic Forum's blog on July 30, 2014, Jeffrey D. Sachs (Professor of Sustainable Development, Professor of Health Policy and Management, Director of the Earth Institute at Columbia University, and Special Adviser to the United Nations Secretary-General on the Millennium

---

[34] http://www.cbc.ca/news/politics/kyoto-climate-change-treaty-sputters-to-a-sorry-end-1.1184986

Development Goals) highlights how 'directed technological change' in which government, scientists, and industry teamed up, led to extraordinary feats of achievement such as the Manhattan Project (to produce the atomic bomb during World War II), the first moon landing, the information technology revolution that has brought us computers, smart phones, GPS and more, the human genome mapping project where the costs of sequencing an individual genome was brought down from around $100 million in 2001 to just $1,000 in about ten years. He argues that despite low carbon emission alternatives being within reach, the push towards truly achieving desired goals lacks intensity and commitment, while carbon dioxide emissions are rising and 'the world is wrecking the climate and food supply systems at a breakneck pace.'[35]

Aart de Zeeuw and Rick van der Ploeg also write in an article published in the same blog on Aug 4, 2014,

---

[35] http://forumblog.org/2014/07/climate-change-technology-jeffrey-sachs/

how most carbon emission impact assessment models do not take into account everything that should be taken into account. The authors point out: "global warming has many non-marginal effects on both the economy and the carbon cycle. Climate catastrophes can occur that lead to sudden flooding, hurricanes, desertification, water shortages, etc. Many such changes may be irreversible."

"Other catastrophes, such as reversal of the Gulf Stream or sudden release of greenhouse gases from the permafrost, lead to a sudden and long-lasting change in the system dynamics of the carbon cycle. Such changes are called regime shifts, and when they take place it's called a tipping point. Scientists predict that at some point, structural changes will occur with effects that are very difficult or even impossible to reverse. This means that the usual analytical models put us on the wrong track. The problem is much more serious than we think." the authors add.[36]

Another example of lopsided views contaminating public policy-making and tilting it rapidly towards disaster, is the endless cacophony and distortions on inflation and interest rates. In an article published in 'The Economic Times' on 4th October 2013, titled 'Why India's rampant inflation remains a puzzle?'[37], the director general of India's first 'Independent Office of Evaluation', a government mandated advisory body, writes in his personal capacity pointing out various factors contributing to India's persistently high and rising inflation, reaching the highest among all emerging economies where in contrast it has fallen.

---

[36] http://forumblog.org/2014/08/climate-tipping-point-carbon-emissions/

[37] http://economictimes.indiatimes.com/opinion/comments-analysis/why-indias-rampant-inflation-remains-a-puzzle/articleshow/23477522.cms

The author argued that the Central Bank's (RBI's) "tight monetary policy will only hurt growth without helping control inflation", pointing out that the RBI should not have increased the repo rate in its recent monetary policy announcement, despite concerns over inflation. He supported the criticism by many experts and business groups who asserted that inflation is related to supply-side factors - especially in the food sector, for which tight monetary policy is not the solution.

The author explained that food inflation is high and rising because procurement price for cereals had risen more than the increase in production cost over the last five years (2008-13), which doubled the food subsidy in the same period and may rise further due the implementation of the new food-security law. In addition, higher procurement prices also increased open market prices. Further, he pointed out that the government, instead of releasing the procured food grains in the domestic market, exported it at higher prices, thereby choking domestic supply causing prices to rise. In short, the argument put forward was that the government paying more for buying food grains from farmers coupled with selling the same food at subsidized rates to the country's poor, instead of releasing food-stocks to bring down market prices, increases the fiscal deficit and feeds inflation.

The question that arises here is, had the excess procurement been released in the open market to reduce prices, would the benefit of lower market prices actually have reached the same beneficiaries that the food-security law intended? Instead of relying on market economics to produce the trickle-down effect, whose failure has ample evidence, if the needy are directly benefited and the cost of subsidy recovered by the government - if not fully, at least in part through higher export prices, is it not more socially equitable economics?

The second reason for food inflation put forward by the author was shortage of farm labor and consequent higher wages due to the government's National Rural Employment Guarantee programme (NREGA). While improvement in wages reduced rural poverty, it contributed to higher costs of production. The author proposed less-labor-intensive methods of production to counter the higher rural wages.

It is baffling to note that while the author argued that procurement prices of food grains had increased more than the increase in cost of production, implying beneficial effect to the producer, he complains about higher wage costs even though it has helped reduce rural poverty. On top of that, it is difficult to imagine how replacing manual labor with mechanization will reduce production costs. Will the cost per unit of output be lower in that case, after taking into account the social cost of displaced farm labour? Is it not dangerous to believe that by lowering wages and consequently procurement prices, it would bring down inflation by reversing what is apparently being argued as a food price rise spiral? In a country where the bulk of aggregate demand begins in the rural economy and cascades upwards, in turn generating secondary demand for industrial goods, coupled with the fact that agricultural incomes are highly uncertain by virtue of being monsoon dependent among other reasons, does forcing the rural economy into a low-wage-low-income trap provide the force of aggregate demand that boosts economic growth, and fulfills socio-economic goals of inclusiveness and reducing income disparities?

Attempting to keep manufacturing costs low by employing unskilled labor displaced from a shrinking agricultural activity and migrating into urban areas, is artificial suppression, similar to the industry's persistent hankering for lowering interest rates despite high inflation.

According to the data from National Sample Survey Organisation (NSSO) reported by The Economic Times (Jun 21, 2013)[38], the proportion of agricultural workforce has fallen below 50% for the first time from 63% in 2009-10, to 49% by 2011-12. A fall of 14 percentage points in merely two years is in itself quite alarming. This is in addition to the fact that the proportion of total population joining the workforce came down from 43% in 2004-05 to 39.5% in 2011-12, even though much of the fall is contributed by women. For men, the proportion was steady at nearly 56%. The NSSO argues that the fall in women entering employment could be because they stayed longer in the education phase. However what the report is missing is that this could also be because of the fall in agricultural activity and the resultant migration of men to urban areas that renders female farm hands obsolete. Most women in rural regions work as helping hands to the men in fields. All this is

[38] http://articles.economictimes.indiatimes.com/2013-06-21/news/40119458_1_demographic-dividend-workforce-labour-force-participation-rate

nothing short of disaster, but the NSSO report labels the fall in agri-workforce as 'progress' and that even the 49% is 'still way too high'. It is not as if manual agriculture has been replaced with mechanized agriculture or that agricultural productivity has dramatically increased, rendering farm labor surplus in agriculture and better employed elsewhere.

Even while this deformity is taking place, experts continue to believe and advise that 'India must leave behind agriculture, family companies and public sector monoliths for competitive, professionally run enterprises', of course adding hope with their apparent belief that this should be accompanied by massive development in agricultural research and development, infrastructure and mechanization.[39] Hopefully, policy makers should not equate 'urbanisation' with 'development' and expect displaced agri-workforce, devoid of industrial skills, to be absorbed to produce low-cost industrial goods.

[39] http://www.business-standard.com/article/opinion/towards-2050-structural-shifts-113062400043_1.html

After all someone, somehow must produce food, unless we believe other countries will fulfill that need, allowing us to import from them and our own labor will be transformed into highly-trained and highly-paid factory hands! So, we become dependent rather than being self-sufficient even for food. Worse, imagine the outcome if every country follows this rationale! If urbanization was the panacea for socio-economic progress, then where will the world get its food from? Manufacture it in factories?

Would the industry push itself, the government and its advisors to look beyond 'urbanization' as the panacea for the economy's evils? Far from that, even well researched and sensible advice from stalwarts like Dr. Amartya Sen[40], is discarded as retrograde and likened to 'putting the cart before the horse' by other economists[41] holding contrasting views.

---

[40] http://articles.economictimes.indiatimes.com/2013-08-03/news/41033908_1_growth-spurts-amartya-sen-prosperity
[41]
http://www.livemint.com/Opinion/9Qzg05zypjEUbioqK9N1UM/Why-Amartya-Sen-is-wrong.html

With food insecurity looming large due to climate change, there no doubt that self sufficiency in food will be a great source of economic strength in the years to come. In this scenario, abandoning agriculture and believing only in industrialization as the vehicle for economic prosperity is a preposterous and ominous thought that will only invite disaster. The Food and Agricultural Organisation of the United Nations (FAO), in its 2009 report, 'The State of Food Insecurity in the World' said "even before the food crisis and the economic crisis, the number of hungry people had been increasing slowly but steadily. With the onset of these crises, however, the number of hungry people in the world increased sharply. As a result, poor households have been forced to eat fewer meals and less-nutritious food, cut back on health and education expenses, and sell their assets. Despite the financial constraints faced by governments around the world, agricultural investment and safety nets remain key parts of an effective response to reduce food insecurity both now and in the future."[42] The updated 2013 report says "Despite overall progress, marked differences across regions persist. Sub-Saharan Africa remains the region with the highest prevalence of undernourishment, with modest progress in recent years. Western Asia shows no progress, while Southern Asia and Northern Africa show slow progress. Significant reductions in both the estimated number and prevalence of undernourishment have occurred in most countries of Eastern and South Eastern Asia, as well as in Latin America.[43] The World Economic Forum has also identified and reported in its 'Global Risks 2014' report, 'Food Crisis' as one of the top ten of the 31 global risks that are likely to cause significant negative impact for several countries and industries over a time frame of up to 10 years.[44]

---

[42] http://www.fao.org/docrep/012/i0876e/i0876e00.htm
[43] http://www.fao.org/publications/sofi/en/
[44] http://reports.weforum.org/global-risks-2014/

Only a robust agricultural economy will provide the necessary scale for industrial goods by boosting aggregate demand not only in the domestic economy but worldwide. This will enable greater automation, which, coupled with necessary skill building, will improve quality and bring down manufacturing costs of industrial products. This will set a virtuous cycle in motion, as better quality and cheaper industrial products will find both domestic as well as export markets. Higher disposable incomes in the hands of labor coupled with fulfillment of their aspiration needs will also increase savings and investment in a healthy manner, rather than feeding unnecessary speculative bubbles, that artificial suppression of costs - whether wages or interest - have the potential to produce.

A prominent and commendable example of economic transformation through agriculture is Brazil. The Economist reported in a story titled 'The miracle of the cerrado' (Aug 2010), how "in less than

30 years Brazil has turned itself from a food importer into one of the world's great breadbaskets.....Brazil has done all this without much government subsidy. This astonishing transformation matters not only to Brazil but also to the rest of the world."[45]

While policy makers in India believe that the alarming fall in agricultural workforce (implying activity) from 63% to 49% in a short span of two years is 'progress', and expert advisors equating urbanization with economic development, China tells a different story. "With comparatively little agricultural land and water resources, China has made food security and self sufficiency in the key food crops of rice and wheat a top policy priority. The government has instituted a policy to prevent any further exit of land from agriculture" according to the 'OECD-FAO Agricultural Outlook 2013-22'

---

[45] http://www.economist.com/node/16886442

report.[46]. Both Brazil (rank 85) and China (rank 101) stand higher on the Human Development Index as of 2012 compared to India at 136.

It is myopic to grumble about higher farm wages, higher procurement prices and poor distribution as contributing to food inflation, while the real issue of impending food shortage due to exit from agriculture receives scant attention. Self-sufficiency in food cannot happen unless farming is strengthened by better methods and improved storage facilities within the control of the farming community so as to prevent their exploitation by unscrupulous middle-men and migration in search of urban jobs as unskilled labor. Annual loss in food grains in India due to lack of adequate storage facilities is a staggering ₹440 billion (₹44,000 crore).[47] In fact as the Economic Survey 2013 (p.91) itself confesses, "While the Food Corporation of

[46] http://www.oecd.org/site/oecd-faoagriculturaloutlook/china-2013.htm
[47] http://www.business-standard.com/article/economy-policy/food-items-worth-rs-44-000-crore-go-waste-every-year-113082300516_1.html

India (FCI) has undertaken open market sales for domestic use and exports, these operations have so far had limited impact on domestic prices."[48] The reason being, most of the open market sales were mopped up by large traders for sale in the domestic as well as the export market, which validates the previous argument on this point.

If storage and distribution systems do not improve, and if interest rates are artificially reduced despite stubborn food driven inflation, it will only create undesirable side-effects. Savings, unable to beat inflation due to inadequate interest, will find its way into other assets mostly real estate, equity and gold. This will spur excess speculation and create asset bubbles. It will also encourage hoarding of food crops to rig up prices driven by the need to earn more to counter the effect of low interest and high inflation. Looking at interest rates only from the

---

[48] http://indiabudget.nic.in/es2012-13/echap-04.pdf

industry's perspective is lopsided economics which will only have adverse consequences.

Incidentally, if we believe in the flawed notion that 'cheap labor' and 'weak currency' is a competitive advantage for India, resulting in low production cost and higher export earnings respectively, the remark made by one of the international automobile manufacturers should be an eye-opener. "India is now one of the cheapest places in the world because the Rupee is sliding while the Chinese Renminbi is getting stronger so it is good for production and export. Although there are some components, particularly electronics, which can only be sourced from China, in other respects it has made Indian components more competitive."[49] Competitive? Only because it's cheap and therefore benefits the industry?

---

[49] http://timesofindia.indiatimes.com/business/india-business/India-turns-sourcing-favourite-for-auto-companies/articleshow/21152613.cms

How does one explain that despite its strong currency and rising labor cost[50], China remains the favored destination for hi-tech products? The Renminbi has steadily strengthened clocking 6.8, 6.8, 6.5, 6.3 and 6.2 to a dollar in the last four years (2009-13) whereas the Rupee has declined. It was 48.4 in 2009 strengthening only in 2010 to 45.7 and sliding rapidly to 46.7, 53.4 and 58.6 in 2011, 2012 and 2013 respectively. And while we believe high wages to be the cause of food-grain driven inflation, China's consumer price inflation for 2011, 2012 and 2013 has been trending down at 5.4%, 2.7% and 2.6% respectively despite rising labor costs[51] and India has seen a rise with 8.9%, 9.3% and 10.9% for the same period, according to the World Bank database.[52] Low labor cost per capita cannot be a correct yardstick for measuring competitiveness, higher efficiency is. Higher efficiency in farming can

[50] http://www.bloomberg.com/news/2014-01-06/china-wages-seen-jumping-in-2014-amid-shift-to-services-.html

[51] http://www.vancouversun.com/Business/asia-pacific/Thinktank+cheap+rice+over+rising+farm+wages+could/8793686/story.html

[52] http://databank.worldbank.org/data/views/reports/tableview.aspx#

only come from better methods, more organized farming, better irrigation, crop protection and more importantly adequate storage and efficient distribution to reduce wastage, pilferage and exploitation of farmers. Only providing 'subsidised inputs' - seeds, fertilizers, credit etc - without rectifying structural defects, is like buying more life insurance and not paying attention to maintaining good health. Low wages only disturbs and weakens the demand-supply-consumption-savings-investment cycle. It doesn't require esoteric economic knowledge to understand this simple equation.

Albert Einstein had rightly defined insanity as "doing the same thing over and over again and expecting different results". Knowing that the 'trickle-down' effect of capitalism has not really happened the way it was envisaged in more than two centuries, if we still refuse to do things differently, there can be no better word to describe us.

No less alarming - and rather intrinsically connected with food security - is management of water resources. Water crisis has been ranked 3rd among the top ten global risks the world would confront in the next 10 years, according to the World Economic Forum's 'Global Risks 2014' report.[53] In fact it has been classified as 'high impact and high likelihood', because of its direct as well as indirect effect on the environment and food production.

Highlighting "the devastating impacts of having too little water or too much" the report says "In 2010, floods in Pakistan paralysed large parts of the country for many weeks, killing thousands of people and wrecking the rural economy. Thailand's slow-onset flood in 2011 caused fewer deaths but showed how one local event could have an impact across the world: global car production slowed as supplies of components were cut, and hard-drive manufacture for the world's computers was slashed. Similarly,

---

[53] http://reports.weforum.org/global-risks-2014/

Japan's GDP and global industrial production dipped significantly following the tsunami of March 2011."

"Too little water can also have systemic impacts. Drought in Russia in 2010 led to restrictions on agricultural exports, causing the price of staple grains to rise across North Africa and the Middle East. The resulting food shortages and price rises aggravated the tensions that led to the Arab Spring. Some studies suggest that water scarcity could reduce grain production by as much as 30%."

"In the future, geopolitical tensions over access to strategic water resources could become more systemically impactful, and water shortage coupled with poverty and societal instability could weaken intra-state cohesion......any failings in its planning, management and use in one country can ripple across the world. That management is becoming increasingly complex and difficult as populations expand and people grow wealthier, demanding more freshwater to supply cities and factories and consuming more foods, such as dairy and meat that need more water to produce."

"Water is equally key for energy production. While the world population grew fourfold in the 20th century, freshwater withdrawals grew nine times."

"Drought and flood could increasingly ravage the economies of poorer countries, locking them more deeply into cycles of poverty"

"Pollution incidents have paralysed business operations in parts of China and elsewhere, disrupting global value chains and damaging corporate reputations – poor water quality or shortages are often blamed on business operations even when businesses comply fully with regulatory requirements."

"How can the global community respond? The overarching prescription is for a package of investments in information, institutions and infrastructure. But successful water management needs the cooperation of a wide network of water users, public and private institutions."

Another matter of grave concern is education. The Hindu (Apr 13, 2013) reports about India that "with eight million children never having stepped inside a school and 80 million dropping out without completing basic schooling, the United Nations Children's Fund has described the situation as a national emergency" Despite the implementation of Right to Education Act 2009 in the past three years "children are dropping out, not for labor, but because they are not learning anything in schools," Louis-Georges Arsenault, UNICEF Representative in India, said. In a visible demonstration of defensiveness in face of national embarrassment, the Vice-Chancellor of the National University of

Educational Planning and Administration drew attention to 'quantity' saying that the number of enrolments increased by 11.18 million in three years, dropout rate came down to 27% and 41% at primary and elementary level respectively, and pupil-teacher ratio had improved across most States, even as the UNICEF representative added that "the focus has to be on improving the quality and way of teaching because poor outcomes are a result of poor schooling and poor teaching."

The Chairperson of National Commission for Protection of Child Rights pointed out that a survey covering 300 districts showed there were no language teachers in 37%, no social-studies teachers in 31% and no maths and science teachers in 29%.[54]

School drop-out not only adds to poorly educated citizens, but also gives rise to deterioration in social character, poor values and vulnerability to anti-social

[54] http://www.thehindu.com/news/national/out-of-school-children-and-dropout-a-national-emergency-unicef/article4611287.ece

activities; and as these children progress into adulthood, under-employment and joblessness, resulting in frustration and moral retardation contributing to more crimes. The National Crime Records Bureau (NCRB) data shows that in 10 years to 2012, there was a 143% increase in the number of rapes by juveniles, 87% increase in murders committed by minors, 500% increase in the number of kidnappings of women and girls by minors.[55]

Lawyer and Social Activist Flavia Agnes rightly emphasizes that "juvenile crime is a reflection of a break down in our society. The onus is on society to rehabilitate the child. Many of these kids come from single parent homes. Often there is no father, so the kids become school dropouts and their mother is at work whole day trying to make ends meet and what does the child do? They run errands for drug addicts for bootlegging, petty theft, selling stuff procured through theft. This is the training ground. So here

---

[55] http://www.ndtv.com/article/india/heinous-crimes-by-minors-on-the-rise-shows-ncrb-data-415367

we are creating a society of young juvenile prostitutes, young juvenile criminals and saying give them death penalty, give them life imprisonment, give them stringent punishment. Okay, so we punish 10, 20, 100, are we going to have a better society?"

Private businesses can easily set-up and manage schools. If telecom, power, banking and aviation sectors can be privatized, why can't education (not mere literacy)? Isn't strong human capital a vital infrastructure for a strong economy? Not the way it has been turned into lucrative profiteering business by some, but by setting up professionally run, fully funded or public-private partnership institutions with the right goals. In addition, the private sector can influence sound policy framework and regulations for private education to prevent profiteering and ensure that inclusiveness in education is truly achieved and does not stop at mere literacy. The irony in unaided private schools as they exist is, while fee revenues are the management's discretion, teachers' salaries are linked with government pay-scales. If teachers are not available in government schools at the salaries that are paid, one can imagine the state of affairs in private education.

You can't have a strong nation and economy with poorly educated citizens. Lack of education leads to poor awareness, undeveloped reasoning abilities and coupled with economic backwardness makes people vulnerable to exploitation by vested interests. Gullible, unaware populace elects wrong leaders, setting off a vicious cycle of poor governance, poor economy, corruption, crime, communal conflicts and other social evils. A democracy cannot survive on decentralizing public governance and decision making alone, such as what is vehemently advocated by some social activists. It must be backed by aware populace. Merely decentralizing governance and authority without enhancing the ability of the masses to reason and judge will only lead to impulsive, fanatic, orthodox, superstition-driven decisions and governance, worsening the socio-economic structure by each passing day. Evidence of faulty reasoning and wrong decision making at lower levels of judiciary, shifting and increasing the burden on the highest authority is already before us. Rabindranath Tagore, had aptly expressed the pressing need for replacing 'habit' with 'reason' for real 'freedom' to work, in one from his Nobel Prize winning collection of poems 'Gitanjali', writing "…….Where the clear stream of reason has not lost its way into the dreary desert sand of dead habit……..Into that heaven of freedom, my Father, let my country awake". Daniel Kahneman also studied and explained how human decision making is influenced by heuristics or mental shortcuts that causes systematic deviations from rational choice, in his well known 'Prospect Theory', for which he was honored with the 2002 Nobel award. The importance of quality in mass education cannot be more emphasized.

Poor quality of education in India is also reflected in the PISA scores. PISA (Programme for International Student Assessment) is a global study conducted by Organisation for Economic Cooperation and Development (OECD) every three years to assess 15-year olds on their performance in math, science and reading. The data helps countries to assess the quality of education and its impact on economic and social well-being.

Even as the scores for 2012 showed China on top, followed by other Asian countries - South Korea, Japan, Taiwan and Macau - India did not participate at all, blaming the test to be 'disconnected' with what was taught in schools. This was after India ranked 73 out of 74 nations in the 2009 study.

While PISA scores are intended to urge governments in different countries to introspect on their education system and improve where necessary, it has been made out to be an inter-country school competition by us, where because participation is voluntary, we don't want to. We don't even want to accept we have a problem. Solving it is a far cry[56] Why can't private business develop curriculum for schools and help the government, or support public organizations set up for the purpose?

No matter how and how much we attempt to conceal our flaws, we can't escape reality. Especially when it is measured using a common global yardstick. India's human development rank stands at a pathetic 136 among 186 countries according to the Human Development Report 2013 published by the United Nations Development Programme (UNDP).[57] The human development index (HDI) is a single statistic that serves as a frame of reference for both social and economic development and is a composite measure of health, education and income, as an alternative to purely economic assessments of

---

[56] http://blogs.economictimes.indiatimes.com/therovingeye/entry/pisa-china-tops-india-has-fled-the-race
[57] https://data.undp.org/dataset/Table-1-Human-Development-Index-and-its-components/wxub-qc5k

national progress, such as GDP growth. Even if we attribute the low rank to any number of factors, the fact that countries like Philippines(114), Indonesia(121), South Africa(121), Vietnam(127), Iraq(131) rank higher and other BRIC countries China at 101, Brazil at 85 and Russian Federation at 55 being way above, shows we have a long way to go.

If we - both private enterprise and the government together - don't do the right things to strengthen our own economy, we have no one to blame except ourselves, when the inevitable downward swing of the economic cycle hits us. Looking for 'external factors' as explanations, or expecting others to slow-down because we haven't yet caught up, is mindless whining.

Subir Gokarn, the ex-deputy governor of the Reserve Bank of India, drew attention to this very point in an article titled 'The taper that didn't'

(Business Standard May 12, 2014)[58], referring to the oscillating fiscal stimulus withdrawal decisions of the United States and the associated reactions in emerging economies. Unless structural weaknesses are fixed, the impact of the eventual withdrawal of fiscal stimulus by the U.S. would be severe and long lasting he said. In a connected world, evaluating the global impacts of fiscal-economic decision making becomes imperative. However, one must not be mistaken to believe that the U.S. has been benign to the pleas of the emerging economies, by withholding the stimulus withdrawal. It's very easy to understand this. In India's context, a lower currency value is always attractive for anyone who wants to invest dollars in the country. However a currency on the downhill path is not. The simple reason being, all returns from investments will be wiped off if the rupee weakens by the same or greater degree after making the investment. For example, if $100 are invested at say ₹50 to a dollar, i.e ₹5,000, and the

---

[58] http://www.business-standard.com/article/opinion/subir-gokarn-the-taper-that-didn-t-113092200748_1.html

investment grows by 20% to ₹6,000 in rupee terms, but the rupee weakens to ₹60 to a dollar, in dollar terms there's no real growth in the investment because ₹6000 would translate back to $100 at the new exchange rate. At an exchange rate of ₹65, it would be worse translating to about $92, a loss of 8%.

Logic suggests that, even if the U.S. economy was in fact strengthening, and because of this the U.S. wants to withdraw the fiscal stimulus, problems would arise. The dollars that were invested in India, would want to move back to a now strengthening U.S. economy. Dollar outflows would only weaken the already depreciated rupee further, hurting those invested dollars. It would be natural for the U.S. to weigh the benefits of withdrawing the stimulus, signaling a strengthening economy and thereby motivating dollars to flow back into the country, against the prospective loss of investment value due to further rupee weakening. In this scenario it makes sense for the U.S. to defer the withdrawal of stimulus even if the U.S. economy was on a sound recovery footing - but only for an opportune time - not permanently. Once the return on dollar investments (mostly in equities) exceeds potential fall in exchange rate due to stimulus-withdrawal, why wouldn't disinvestment happen?

So, even if the exchange rate is propped up through various monetary policy actions, it becomes irrelevant for the invested dollars. Rather it only helps faster outflows by preventing currency depreciation. All that matters to dollars waiting to move back to a strengthening home country is whether there is net return on investment on the already invested dollars, taking both, returns earned and exchange value lost into account. If artificial supports keep the rupee from weakening, it's better for the foreign investor. It is this window of opportunity during which India has to get its economy into shape, which Subir Gokarn talks about, so that some justification develops for retaining at least some of those dollars - those that are willing to take a reasonable risk - invested in India. The ball is in India's court now, whether to make the dollar's stay in India seem worthwhile or frustrate it to leave the country.

With the variety of consumer 'needs' growing faster than the rise in human population itself - thanks to the contribution of technology in the creation of products and services as well as the media in dissemination of product awareness and influencing lifestyle changes, the explosion of choices available makes it increasingly challenging for consumers to discriminate between genuine, healthy needs, and sensory perceptions created by advertising and marketing blitzkrieg. While this phenomenon is happening, the tussle between companies for extracting maximum mileage from laissez faire - mostly focusing on short term as well as a narrow perspective, rather than a longer term larger picture -

may seem to put business managers and leaders in a quandary.

Private enterprise can play a strong role in strengthening four important pillars of economic well-being and prosperity - education, healthcare, law making and law enforcement. While some of these such as education and healthcare can be boosted by direct participation from private sector - for example setting up fully owned schools from their own funds that provide top-class education either free or at subsidized cost, employing talented teachers and paying them handsomely, (not profiteering). This investment in grass-root human capital formation will pay huge dividends in the long run. Aware, thinking and educated citizens will automatically fuel good governance through doing the right things and choosing leaders who do the right things. Setting up incentivised higher-educational institutes in designated 'backward' areas does nothing to the local economy but only benefits 'educational trusts'; and there's no dearth of 'experts' who help in devising the best 'tax-planning' strategies to those 'trustees'. Think about it - if school drop-out rates are high, where will the higher-education 'intake' come from? It's not that the likes of Harvards and Stanfords are growing by the dozens in India, that international students would be attracted to.

Same can be said about healthcare. Hospitals, dispensaries, diagnostic centres, pharmacies etc owned by the private sector, can provide top class healthcare to the masses as well as promote good health through awareness programmes, on the same lines as education. If mass education and healthcare jobs are well paid, they will attract talent and elevate the status of these jobs in society. If the onus for doing this is taken directly by the private sector, it has the potential to deliver measurable results, rather than leaving it to the hands of many a hoax NGO. On the parallel, private sector can influence right public policy and actions in these two areas through strong representation from industry associations. For instance elevating the salaries (and consequently social status) of government teachers and doctors. The message they send to governments should be - 'we are already doing this, unless you too do this, our long term aggregate demand, our long term economic sustainability is at risk'. Growth in 'Medical tourism' because of 'low-cost' healthcare is no triumph to talk about. It's an embarrassment to the country's healthcare system.

Similarly, law making and law enforcement will be strengthened if private sector supports and promotes those laws that ensure socio-economic justice, rather than lobbying only for the 'industry friendly' ones; complying with regulations honestly rather than finding ways of 'dodging' them. This will automatically boost government revenues, reduce revenue leakages and promote non-corrupt government functioning.

Once this culture permeates throughout the socio-economic system, governments can also channelize revenues in the right direction. For example, raising salaries (and social status) of judiciary and police, so as to attract the country's best talents. It's pointless to blame poor law and order when the law enforcer, struggles to have his own home in order first.

Large retail chains 'selling' plastic bags for carrying the goods which customers buy does nothing to reduce plastic consumption and production. Replacing them with paper, cloth or jute bags is not only environment friendly, but will promote 'green' industry rather than 'toxic' ones. No amount of 'banning' will stop people from consuming toxic products, unless they understand the ill effects and make the right choices through being better educated and more aware.

Nothing can prove the futility of 'banning' than the recent actions on gold imports. When the Indian government was bogged by a rising current account deficit (CAD), they blamed it on 'gold fetish' among Indians, and increased the import duty on gold to curb imports.[59] Did this reduce the demand for gold? While the high-duty policy was announced in the first half of calendar year 2013, there was a four-fold increase in gold smuggling by mid 2014.[60] If the December 2013 news, reported in 'The Economic Times' - "Gold duty hike in India sees higher imports in Pakistan, Bangladesh, Myanmar, Nepal and Sri Lanka" - is to be believed, we can easily see the correlation and where the smuggled gold could be coming from.[61] Tragically, while the CAD was still sad, and the Indian rupee breached a low of 68 to a dollar, the finance ministry called this behaviour 'irrational sentiment'.[62] Sentiment yes, but irrational?

[59] http://www.bloomberg.com/news/2013-08-13/india-increases-gold-tax-for-third-time-this-year-to-cut-deficit.html

[60] http://timesofindia.indiatimes.com/business/india-business/Four-time-jump-in-smuggling-Gold-worth-Rs-245-crore-seized-in-2013-14/articleshow/34966237.cms

[61] http://economictimes.indiatimes.com/markets/commodities/gold-duty-hike-in-india-sees-higher-imports-in-pakistan-bangladesh-myanmar-nepal-and-sri-lanka/articleshow/27314310.cms

[62] http://www.business-standard.com/article/economy-policy/mayaram-calls-the-rupee-fall-irrational-sentiment-113082800779_1.html

What is irrational about poorly educated (as well as illiterate) masses relying on gold and real estate for social security, rather than 'paper' securities which they don't understand, their poor economic health and inadequate social security only exacerbating their fears? What is true about 'ban on gold' is also true about ban on 'plastic', 'ghutka' and so on.

The undeniable truth is that only those who strongly cut through the dilemma and rigidly follow the right ethical path will survive for generations to come; for there have been more people on this planet before us, and more will be after us, to be served by entrepreneurs from the same corporate family! If there is even one thing that distresses us today for which we find fault with our earthly predecessors, then there will probably be multifold things that our successors on this earth may blame us for - unless we think about them now!

Wow! Look at those leaves! Shining aren't they?

5

Strategy:

Caution!

Wet Roads

"We could leave our strategic plan on an airplane, somebody could pick it up, and it wouldn't matter. It's all about execution."
- John Stumpf, CEO - Wells Fargo

Strategy is the binding glue that connects the four intents imperative for entrepreneurial success - caring for employees, caring for customers, caring for society and caring for the planet - to action. Yet, a majority of business organizations are unable to make their strategies work. According to the research findings of Dr. John Kotter, Professor

Emeritus at Harvard Business School, which has been validated by several other studies, "approximately 5% of all organizations implement their strategies successfully, and 70% of strategic initiatives fail to meet their objectives. The remaining 25% have some middling success but do not meet the full potential of the strategy devised." (Forbes Oct 2012).[1] Why do strategies fail?

Conventionally, much of the learning about business strategy as well as some operational tools has been based on parallels drawn from battles and war. Yet, the greatest irony of war is that it is used as a weapon to achieve peace! Does it? Should it be any different in business? So, the hard-wired reference point for business strategy must first be 'unlearnt'. The notion of business as a war between competitors is in itself the cause of failed strategies. Three distinguished professors at Harvard Business School - Michael Porter, Jan Rivkin and Rosabeth

---

[1] Dr. John Kotter, the Konosuke Matsushita Professor of Leadership, Emeritus at Harvard Business School.

Moss Kanter did a study on American competitiveness beginning in 2011. They interviewed 6,000 Harvard Business School Alumni, of which nearly a third held top leadership positions, from every sector of the economy. The results reported in a book titled 'Competitiveness at the Crossroads', were astonishing. While most perceived that the quality of their own management was not a problem, American firms lost out on global competitiveness. Faulty management actions learnt from B Schools caused "serious social problems (loss of jobs, stagnating income, growing inequality) and eventually a decline of the public sector.[2] Why did this happen?

The key factors that contribute to strategy failures could be wrapped in a nutshell as follows:

a) Excessive pre-occupation with competitors rather than customers. "So I think instead of focusing on

---

[2] http://www.forbes.com/sites/stevedenning/2013/03/10/the-surprising-reasons-why-america-lost-its-ability-to-compete/

the competition, focus on the customer" says Scott Cook, Co-Founder, Director and Chairman of Executive Committee, Intuit Inc. Quite right, it's one thing to be aware of what competitors are doing, but what is more important is knowing how competitors understand the customer. The biggest blunder would be assuming that competitors' understanding of customers is right, and therefore their actions, and then retaliating. Instead, greater amount of intelligent effort in reading the customers' mind - going beyond standard superficial marketing surveys - would give you a cutting edge over competition. Only a correctly oriented front-end customer interface team can achieve that. Essentially this means keeping them focused on the customer and not sales targets. Knowing the right thing is everything. That would keep the strategic mission and vision, the very essence of 'being in business', always in forefront.

Take the reaction by Colgate India when Procter & Gamble (P&G) launched Oral-B toothpaste in July 2013. Heaps of Colgate toothpaste packs suddenly flooded shelf space at leading supermarkets with buy one get one, reduced price offers and freebies, to edge P&G out, in a frenzied bombarding.[3] Did Colgate do the right thing? It may seem so to most who are tuned to the battle-field conditioning. It would have also become the favorite topic of conversation in corporate corridors and food for B-School marketing case studies.

Let's look at it differently. If we compare the impact both companies made to their respective shareholder value in the equity markets in the period following the event, it appears that Colgate's bulldozing was not worthwhile. After all, the actions of company managements, who are mere agents of shareholders, must result in growth in value of equity capital - in shareholders' wealth.

---

[3] http://articles.economictimes.indiatimes.com/2013-07-12/news/40536812_1_colgate-prabha-parameswaran-toothpaste

According to equity price data from the National Stock Exchange, while Colgate's stock price rose from ₹1349 a share on July 1, 2013 to ₹1418 on May 9, 2014, an increase of 5%, Procter & Gamble registered nearly five times the number, a whopping 24% during the same period, rising from ₹2943 to ₹3654 per share.

A look at the financial performance of the two companies explains why the market could have reacted the way it did.

Colgate Palmolive (India)

	Mar 2013	Jun 2013 (Q to Q)	Dec 2013 (Q to Q)
Sales	812	845	884
		(+4%)	(+5%)
A&S Cost	82	101	121
		(+23%)	(+20%)
EBIT	169	171	155
		(+1%)	(- 9%)
EBIT %	21%	20%	18%

Procter and Gamble (India)

	Mar 2013	Jun 2013 (Q to Q)	Dec 2013 (Q to Q)
Sales	417	423	571
		(+1%)	(+35%)
A&S Cost	65	57	98
		(-12%)	(+72%)
EBIT	58	64	88
		(+10%)	(+38%)
EBIT %	14%	15%	15%

While Colgate saw its operating margin deteriorate from 21% to 18%, P&G improved its margin from 14% to 15%, despite a higher proportion of Administrative and Selling expenses at 17% of sales compared to Colgate's 14% for quarter ending Dec 2013. This comparison is too limited to truly understand why P&G's future prospects inspired higher optimism from the market, increasing its market price nearly five times in percentage terms, than Colgate's. Yet it raises questions on the worthiness of what Colgate did. Whether making the competitor's products virtually unavailable by crowding shelf-space is a good strategy? If all competitors engage in this game, where will it lead to in the long term?

Another case is Tata's small car Nano. Definitely extensive pre-launch market research must have been done. Yet the model struggles to attract sales. After spending more than $1 billion in the project, the company sold a total of 242,431 Nanos in four years since its launch in 2009, while the sales forecast made during the launch, was a whopping 250,000 per annum.[4] This is clearly the evidence that something grossly went wrong in understanding what customers want.

b) Ego barriers. The job of understanding the customers correctly is that of the strategic leadership. If this job is not done right, it sets the wrong goals for the rest of the organization to follow. Even if a

---

[4] http://articles.economictimes.indiatimes.com/2013-12-30/news/45711162_1_tata-motors-nano-cheapest-car

course correction is possible during the preliminary phases of gathering intelligence and brainstorming by the frontline executives, strategic leadership can easily scuttle these prospects because of 'ego' barriers. Ego can have powerful negative impact on extracting truly rational outcomes, and seriously impede learning.

c) Poor communication. After assimilating insights into the customers' mind, and going past the 'ego' barrier, the next most important element is powerful communication. Thought leads, action follows. Bridging the two is communication. Clear understanding and clear and open communication leads to correct goal setting and smooth execution. If strategic management falters at this, the rest of the organization would simply crumble, because everyone would align themselves to what the top leadership conveys, overtly or covertly. Blaming such failures on 'poor team-work' is only a lame excuse for what truly should classify as leadership failure.

Ouch!! These shoes hurt! Wonder where we're headed! But better follow quietly, than complain and be called the only 'poor team player'.

The article contributed by Kotter International titled 'Your Corporate Strategy: It Just Doesn't Matter', in Forbes (Dec 2012) brilliantly drives home this point with a conclusion "Get out of your office and get some face-time with your team. Encourage the good, help re-direct the lost, and you'll see real progress"[5]

d) Faulty tools. Nothing is more damaging than using the wrong tools to define goals and measure performance. No public company can deny its ultimate financial goal is that of fulfilling long term shareholder expectations. This 'agency role' cannot be discharged unless shareholder expectations are correctly understood, project appraisals are done accordingly, realistic targets are set and actual performance is measured with the same yardstick as the plan, (just WYDIWYP - What You Do Is What You Plan).

Unfortunately this goal, on which other goals are built, uses tools that have been known and proven to be faulty through thousands of studies, even leading to Nobel Awards being conferred on those who

---

contributed to the research. Ample evidence of wide disparity in their application among different organizations exists. No truly scientific standard is available for financial decision making in a world where accounting standards have made remarkable and continuous progress. Based on a path-breaking research, exactly what ails financial decision making and performance measurement, has been painstakingly analyzed and explained in great detail in the author's book 'The Timeless Essence of Financial Science'.[6]

---

[6] http://valueerodingfallacies.blogspot.in

The Last Word

There's no time as opportune as 'Now' to commit ourselves to the 'Change' we want for a better world, a better future - for us, and for our future generations. But for that, first the 'Change' must come from within. Every entrepreneur must take this oath - voluntarily, without waiting for a formal diktat to comply with, or without thinking of it as 'philanthropy'. It's not charity, it's a moral duty.

As Aristotle said "Knowing yourself is the beginning of all wisdom."

About the author

Rajesh D. Mudholkar is a certified Management Accountant with over three decades of professional experience. He brings his knowledge and insights from several years of MNC work as well as teaching at post-graduate business management programs, into his writings. His book 'The Timeless Essence of Financial Science' documents his path-breaking research that resolves decades old flaws in financial decision making and enterprise value measurement, the root cause of financial crises. He is an alumnus of 'University of Mumbai' and Associate member of ICAI, India's apex statutory body for Cost and Management Accounting. He lives in India.

Email: mudholkar.rajesh@gmail.com

Blogs: http://valueerodingfallacies.blogspot.in

http://the-entrepreneurs-oath.blogspot.in

http://callofreason.blogspot.in